TOBAGO

Clean, Green and Seren

Second Edition

Edited by Arif Ali

HANSIB

Published in the United Kingdom
by Hansib Publications Limited, 2012

Email: info@hansib-books.com
Website: www.hansib.com
Website: www.hansib-books.com

ISBN 978-1-906190-49-1

A catalogue record for this book is available
from the British Library

Endpaper images
Front: Water lilies by Oswin Browne;
Back: Sunset at Pigeon Point by Ian Brierley

Design and production, Hansib Publications Limited
Printed and bound in the United Kingdom

Taking care of Tobago

" ... for the enhancement of the autonomy of the Tobago House of Assembly and the preservation of Tobago's heritage."

Orville London, Chief Secretary, The Tobago House of Assembly

In 1957, the Chief Minister of Trinidad and Tobago, Dr Eric Williams, said: "Tobago is a test case. If Trinidad cannot develop Tobago, its claim to be the principal partner in the West Indies Federation, accepting responsibility of developing smaller islands falls to the grounds. Tobago's development is necessary to illustrate to the West Indies and the world outside our capacity for self government and taking care of our own affairs."

The development of Tobago and its relationship with its sister isle, Trinidad, has occupied the minds of many who struggled to ensure that the voices of the people of Tobago were heard and that there were means by which Tobagonians could 'take care of their own affairs'.

ANR Robinson is one of many who campaigned for the rights of the neglected minority in Tobago. He attained his objective in 1980 when the House of Assembly Act was passed for the purpose of "making better provision for the administration of the island of Tobago and for matters therewith" and its first election held with ANR becoming its first Chairman.

The Assembly comprises of twelve elected Assembly members and four Councillors, three of whom are appointed on the advice of the Chief Secretary and one on the advice of the Minority Leader plus a Presiding Officer who may or may not be an Assembly Member or a Councillor.

The Chief Secretary plus seven other Secretaries make up an Executive Council that is responsible for carrying out the functions of the House of Assembly. The Chief Secretary heads this Executive Council and the Presiding Officer presides over all sittings of the Assembly.

The Assembly itself has two arms – The Legislative and The Executive.

The Legislative arm makes policy decisions with respect to the operations of the Assembly.

The Executive arm of the Assembly is headed by the Chief Secretary in his capacity as leader of the Executive Council, which has individual and collective responsibility for carrying out the functions of the Assembly through the several Divisions arranged for the purpose.

Acknowledgements

"Side by side, not one behind the other"

President Sir Ellis Clarke

This second edition of *Tobago: Clean, Green and Serene* comes seven years after Hansib Publications first published it in 2005. Since then, there have been many developments in Tobago, and the Tourism Department continues to make concerted efforts to increase visitor numbers. Today, there is more accommodation, an improved ferry service, Caribbean Airlines has added night flights, and the 5000-seat Shaw Park Cultural Complex for the arts is near completion, to name but a few. And the journey continues.

The publishing of such a book requires the support of many people, and we were most fortunate to have had such support, especially while working to a very tight production schedule. Grateful thanks are, therefore, due to many individuals and organisations, including the following:

Oswald Williams, Tobago's Secretary of Tourism and Transport, for commissioning the book. The beauty of the island and the hospitality of the people made working there so pleasurable;

Sherma Joanne McDougall-Williams, Avion Hercules, John Arnold and Oswin Browne, without your help and co-operation this book would not have been possible;

Hansib Publications staff and associates who worked and advised on the project in the United Kingdom and Tobago, namely, Managing Editors Kash Ali and Ansel Wong, Richard Painter, Shareef Ali, Alan Cross, Ella Barnes, Anji Benjamin, Justin Joseph, Indul Kanhai and Kendrick Sooknarine;

Rawle Winston Titus, Lawrence Ruiz of Conrado Hotel, Eric Fenient of Coco Reef Hotel, James Solomon, John Wayne Thomas, Vanessa R Williams and the Caribbean Interpreting & Translation Bureau, Ravi and Rishi Rampersad of Ravi Rentals, Dr Michael Belcon for your hospitality and generosity, Cordella Andrews, Dwayne Andrews, Wayne Gregory, Karima Ali-Dookwah of the Cyber Cafe at Grand Bazaar;

Cornell Buckradee, General Manager, Marketing, Tourism Development Company of Trinidad and Tobago;

The photographers (in alphabetical order): Ian Brierley, Stephen Broadbridge, Oswin Browne, Richard Bhagan, Liz Chung, Ryan P. Mannette, Dane Ragbir, Tourism Development Company (TDC), Kyle Walcott.

The contributing writers (in alphabetical order): John Arnold, Michael Belcon, Bertrand Bhikarry, Kwesi DesVignes, Duane Dove, James Fuller, Simon Lee, Dr Adana N. Mahase-Gibson, Leslie Palmer, Caroline Ravello, Sonja Sinaswee, Rev Patricia Stephens, Rawle Winston Titus.

Please forgive me if any names have been inadvertently forgotten.

And finally, thank you to Pamela Mary for caring so much.

Arif Ali
February 2012

Contents

Argyle Falls is located near Roxborough on the Argyle River. At 175 ft (53 m), this three-tiered waterfall is the highest in Tobago and is one of the island's leading attractions. *Photo: Richard Bhagan*

A very beautiful and very special island

The island of Tobago is clean, green and serene. A small largely unspoilt island, Tobago is a destination of first choice for visitors and increasingly, for those investors in the know.

Tobago lies at latitude 11 degrees N, longitude 60 degrees W, 19 miles northeast of its sister island Trinidad. Only 26 miles (41km) long and 7 miles (11km) wide with a landmass of 116 sq miles (300sq km) it is surrounded by coral reefs. The low-lying coralline south west plateau rises gradually to a central ridge of volcanic hills reaching 1,860ft. Dense rainforest (the oldest protected forest in the western hemisphere) rises above the white sand beaches of the Leeward Caribbean coast and the rocky shoreline of the Windward Atlantic.

Until recent geological times Tobago was part of the South American mainland. Its abundant mainland and island flora and fauna include: 220 bird species, 23 butterflies, 24 non-poisonous snakes, 17 bats, 16 lizards, 14 frogs, 12 mammals and 5 marine turtles.

Originally inhabited by Amerindians, Tobago was subsequently contested for by waves of colonising Europeans.

Courlanders arrived first in 1642, followed by the Dutch, French and English, until the island was ceded to Britain by the 1802 Treaty of Paris. Tobago became a British Crown Colony in 1877, joining Trinidad as a political unit in 1888.

The majority of the 54,000 population are descendants of enslaved Africans imported to work the sugar plantations from the late 17th century onwards. Afro-Creole cultural roots survive in folklore, music and cuisine, showcased in the many Festivals throughout the year.

It is the island's rich colonial history, stunning natural resources and unique culture that set it apart from other tourist destinations. Coupled with well-kept facilities, genuinely friendly people and an accessible airport, Tobago is open for business to the whole world.

Visitors will enjoy two rainforests - the "rainforest of the sea" and the "rainforest of the land".

The island is the southeast Caribbean's premier dive location. Gently sloping coral reefs, plunging submarine cliffs and volcanic formations offer exhilarating dives. Nutrient-rich waters teem with

Shopping complex at Pigeon Point
Photo: Ian Brierley

With its long stretch of white sand, Pigeon Point is considered to be Tobago's most beautiful beach. The resort area has excellent facilities including bars, a restaurant, souvenir shops, furniture hire and water sports shops. The thatched-roof jetty has become an internationally recognised icon of Tobago. *Photo: Ian Brierley*

Goat Island (in the foreground) and Little Tobago are located approximately 2.4km off the north-eastern coast of Tobago. Also known as Bird of Paradise Island, Little Tobago is an important breeding site for sea birds such as the red-billed tropicbird. The building seen on Goat Island is the former home of 'James Bond' creator, Ian Fleming. *Photo: Oswin Browne*

Bloody Bay is a sheltered bay with a long, golden-sand beach. *Photo: Oswin Browne*

Snorkellers soon discover that Tobago has some of the best coral reefs in the Caribbean. *Photo: Dane Ragbir*

Stone Haven Bay near Black Rock
Photo: Oswin Browne

nearly 300 species of hard coral; a wide variety of sponges; myriad tropical fishes; whales, sharks, dolphins, rare manta rays, squid and turtles.

The little fishing village of Speyside is dive central, with a diversity of sites and the vortex of tidal streams around the offshore islands, ideal for drift dives. The dive industry is operated to international safety standards, with a free decompression chamber facility in Scarborough.

Different locations cater for the complete range of water sports from sailing, power boat racing, kite surfing and game fishing; those who prefer a more leisurely approach will appreciate reef spotting through glass-bottomed boats, particularly at the Nylon Pool, a shallow aquamarine area created by an off-shore sandbank at Buccoo Reef.

The "rainforest of the land" is a virtual nirvana for naturalists that attracts ornithologists, naturalists and eco tourists eager to sight the emblematic cocrico, hike through the Forest Reserve, scale waterfalls or watch turtles nesting on the beach at night. For the energetically adventurous, mountain biking off road and on, is an excellent alternative to

For all the serenity, visitors will still find a surprisingly full entertainment schedule and nightlife which often showcases local culture. The weekly Sunday School beach party at Buccoo has become an institution, as have the unique Easter goat and crab races. Tobago also stages several Festivals and international events that include Food Festivals, Kite Flying, Drumming, Fashion and Jazz.

The economy, until recently mostly driven by tourism and real estate, is diversifying with light industrial projects like the Cove-Eco Industrial and Business Park and the resuscitation of the former cocoa industry at the Tobago Cocoa Estate near Roxborough.

Real estate development is actively encouraged with investment incentives which have contributed to the many new developments, including large hotel complexes, villa developments and two new malls.

Visitors looking to invest in Tobago benefit not only from these exemptions but the real estate quota, which allows them to own up to five acres of land for commercial purposes, without resident status.

Tobago is a very beautiful and a very

The Nylon Pool is an area of shallow, crystal clear water at Buccoo Reef. Trips to the reef in glass-bottom boats and bathing are popular activities. *Photo: Oswin Browne*

Tobago beckons you to come
and make your own footprints
Photo: Stephen Broadbridge

Pirates Bay
Photo: Oswin Browne

Charlotteville is located at Man O War Bay on the north-eastern coast
Photo: Stephen Broadbridge

Parlatuvier Bay
Photo: Oswin Browne

Pigeon Point
Photo: Stephen Broadbridge

LEGEND

~ Claude Noel Hwy.

— Main Roads

— Other Roads

〜 Rivers & Streams

◑ Bathing Beaches

✈ Airport

⛽ Petrol Station

◣ Dive Sites

❶ Fort Milford

❷ Tourism Info Office

❸ Kimme Museum

❹ Fort Bennet

❺ Adventure Farm

❻ Mason Falls

❼ Fort George

❽ Genesis Nature Park

❾ Richmond Great House

❿ Argyle Falls

⓫ Louis D'Or Nurseries

CARIBBEAN

S

Englishm

Little Engli

Castara Bay

Castara

North

Castara River

Mt. Dillon R.

Castara Down R.

Coffe River

Celery Bay

Gordon Bay

King Peters Bay

Washerwomen's Bay

Little Bay

Moriah

River

ST. DAVID

Culloden Bay

Anse Fromager

Les Coteaux

Arnos Vale Road

Providence

River

Mason Hall

Easterfield River

East

Road

ST. GEORGE

Arnos Vale Bay

Back Bay

❺ Arnos Vale

Franklyn

Arnos Vale Road

❻

Plymouth

Courland Point

G

Great Courland Bay

Courland

Courland River

Plymouth Road

Road

Providence River

Northside Road

Belmont Road

West

Black Rock

Hawks Bill

Black Rock

Lower Quarter or Roselle

Mary's Hill

The Whim

Adelphi

Sandy

Providence

Cinnamon Hill

Bacolet

Hillsborough

Mo

St. G

Stone Haven Bay

❹

Grange

Orange Hill

Orange Hill Road

Rockly Vale

Morne Quinton

Hope

Hillsborough Bay

Mt. Irvine Bay

Bethel

❸

Patience Hill

Lambeau

Steele River

Claude Noel Hwy.

Scarborough

Wolf Rock

Booby Point

Buccoo

❼

Bacolet River

Buccoo Reef

Buccoo Bay

Prospect

Diamond

Harbour

Rockly Bay

Windward

Sheerbirds Point

Auchenskeoch

Buccoo Road

Buccoo

Bay

Road

Highway

Lambeau

Red Point

Bacolet Bay

Minister Point

Pigeon Point

Bon Accord Lagoon

ST. PATRICK

Golden Grove Road

Shirvan

Noel

Claude

Bacolet Point

Milford Bay

Canaan

Milford Road

Little Rockly Bay

Store Bay

❶

Tyson Hall

Kilgwyn

Lowlands

A

❷

Sandy Point

La Guira

Friendship

Brown's or Crown Pt.

Cove

Canoe Bay

Lowlands

Petit Trou

Columbus or Kennedy's Pt.

An idyllic Caribbean scene
Photo: Stephen Broadbridge

THE NATIONAL FLAG

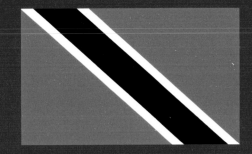

The national flag of Trinidad and Tobago was first used in 1962 when the nation gained its independence. Designed by the late George Bailey, it is made up of a black stripe bordered in white on a red background, each colour representing an element in the character of its land and people.

RED represents the vitality of the land, the warmth and energy of the sun and the courage and friendliness of its people.

WHITE represents the sea which surrounds the land, the cradle of its heritage, the purity of its aspirations and the equality of its people under the sun.

BLACK represents the dedication of the people joined together by one strong bond. It is the colour of strength, of unity, of purpose and of the wealth of the land.

The colours were chosen to represent the elements Earth, Fire and Water and to encompass the nation's past, present and future and to inspire it as one united, vital, free and dedicated people.

THE NATIONAL PLEDGE

I solemnly pledge to dedicate my life
To the service of my God
And to my country.

I will honour my parents,
My teachers, my leaders and my elders,
And those in authority.

I will be clean and honest in all my thoughts,
My words and my deeds.

I will strive, in everything I do
To work together with my fellowmen
Of every creed and race
For the greater happiness of all
And the honour and glory
Of my country.

Written by Marjorie Padmore

THE COAT OF ARMS

The Coat of Arms was designed by the late George Bailey and was first used following independence in 1962.

They show at the top a coconut palm in fruit and a ship's wheel representing the nation's colonial past. The national birds of the country - the Scarlet Ibis (found in Trinidad) and the Cocrico (found only in Tobago) - hold up the shield on which two Hummingbirds, another national bird, are depicted. Also on the shield are three Spanish galleons, the principal motifs of Trinidad and Tobago's British colonial seals. They all stand on three hills which represent the Trinity.

The national watchwords, "Together We Aspire, Together We Achieve" form the base on which the insignia stands.
Photo (below): Ian Brierley

THE NATIONAL FLOWER

Tobago shares its national flower, the Chaconia (*Warszewiczia Coccinea*), with its sister island Trinidad.

Also known as the 'Pride of Trinidad and Tobago' or a 'Wild Poinsettia', the Chaconia was named in honour of the last Spanish Governor of Trinidad, Don Jose Maria Chacon (1784-1797). This wild, forest flower is indigenous to the island and has long sprays of magnificent vermilion that are said to bloom around the anniversary of Trinidad and Tobago's Independence Day (August 31).
Photo (left): Stephen Broadbridge

INTRO (GRANDLY)

FORGED FROM THE LOVE OF LIB—ER—TY, IN THE FIRES OF HOPE AND

PRAYER, WITH BOUND—LESS FAITH IN OUR DES—TI—NY, WE

SOL— EMN —LY DE—CLARE: SIDE BY SIDE WE

STAND ISLANDS OF THE BLUE CA—RIB—BEAN SEA.

THIS OUR NATIVE LAND,— WE PLEDGE OUR LIVES TO THEE. HERE EV'RY

CREED AND RACE FIND AN E— QUAL PLACE, AND MAY GOD — BLESS OUR

NATION.— HERE EV'RY CREED AND RACE FIND AN

E— QUAL PLACE, AND MAY GOD BLESS OUR NA—TION.

THE NATIONAL SEAL

The National Seal dates back to 1815 and the words *Pulchrior evenit*, "She emerges more beautiful", represent Tobago's development nearly two hundred years later.

Officially known as the 'Great Seal and Seal at Arms' it is used as the seal of the Tobago House of Assembly, the local governing administration.

The current seal is a revised modern version of its ancestor, showing four ships sailing in the island's open harbour, a fruit laden coconut tree waving in the breeze and the sun rising over a hill. It is displayed in all government offices and on all official flags and documents.

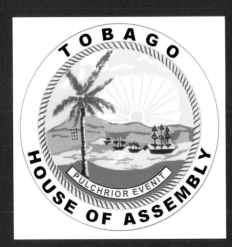

THE NATIONAL BIRD

Tobago's national bird is the Cocrico (*Ortalis ruficauda*) or Rufous-vented Chachalaca.

Known locally as a Tobago Pheasant, it can be heard sounding a loud, grating chorus at dawn and dusk. It stands approximately 55cm (22 inches) tall and mainly inhabits the higher areas amidst the forest feeding on berries and small fruits.
Photo (above): Liz Chung

THE NATIONAL ANTHEM

Forged from the love of liberty
in the fires of hope and prayer
with boundless faith in our destiny
We solemnly declare

Side by side we stand
Islands of the blue Caribbean Sea
This our native land
we pledge our lives to thee

Here every creed and race
find an equal place
And may God bless our nation

Here every creed and race
find an equal place
And may God bless our nation.

Written by Patrick S. Castagne

TOBAGO FACTS & FIGURES

Location
Tobago is the smaller of the two islands that make up the Republic of Trinidad and Tobago. The island occupies an area of 300 sq km (116 sq mi) and lies 30km (19 miles) north-east of Trinidad. It is surrounded by the Caribbean Sea on its north coast and the Atlantic Ocean on its southern and western coasts.

Topography
Tobago is an undulating mass of coral and volcanic rock. The Main Ridge Forest Reserve, Tobago's backbone, is a hilly range of forest which covers 60% of the island. Pigeon Peak, at 549 metres (1801 ft), is its highest point.

Climate
Warm tropical climate with constant cool breezes from NE Trade Winds. Year-round temperatures from 23°C (73°F) to 32°C (89°F). Dry Season: January to June; Wet Season: July to December.

Population / People
Population 54,000 est. About 90% of the population is of African descent with smaller communities of Indian and Middle Eastern descent.

Language
English, but a Tobago Creole is widely spoken.

Capital
Scarborough. Population just over 17,000.

Government
The Tobago House of Assembly carries out local Government duties. There are two Parliamentary seats: Tobago East and Tobago West. The island is divided into seven parishes – Western Tobago: St Andrew, St Patrick and St David; Eastern Tobago: St George, St Mary, St Paul and St John.

Time Zone
Tobago lies in the Atlantic Standard Time Zone which is one hour ahead of US Eastern Standard Time and four hours behind Greenwich Mean Time. There is no Daylight Saving Time.

Electricity
110v/220v. European visitors are required to use an adaptor.

Currency
Trinidad and Tobago (TT) dollar (TT$ = 100 cents). The TT Dollar is tied to the US Dollar and floating at US$1 = TT$6.40. The exchange rate for other major currencies is approximately: £1.00 to TT$10.68; •1 to TT$8.63.

NATIONAL HOLIDAYS

New Year's Day
JANUARY 1. Celebrating the first day of the New Year/ Gregorian calendar

Carnival
FEBRUARY-MARCH. Though not a public holiday, most offices are closed on the two Carnival days – always the Monday and Tuesday before Ash Wednesday

Easter
VARIABLE. Good Friday and Easter mark the death and resurrection of Jesus Christ

Spiritual Shouter Baptist Day
MARCH 30. Commemorating the Shouter Baptist faith

Corpus Christi
VARIABLE. Christian feast in honour of the Holy Eucharist

Indian Arrival Day
MAY 30. Commemorating the arrival of labourers from India under an indentureship scheme

Labour Day
JUNE 19. Marking the labour uprising of June 1937

Emancipation Day
AUGUST 1. Commemorating the emancipation of enslaved peoples

Independence Day
AUGUST 31. Trinidad and Tobago became a Sovereign State

Republic Day
SEPTEMBER 24. Trinidad and Tobago became a Republic

Eid-ul-Fitr
VARIABLE. The end of the Muslim fasting month of Ramadan

Diwali
VARIABLE. Celebrating the Hindu Festival of Lights

Christmas
DECEMBER 25. The Christian celebration of the birth of Jesus Christ

Boxing Day
DECEMBER 26. A public holiday of a gift-giving tradition

TOBAGO TIMELINE

Circa 15,000 – 1,000 BC
Tobago is part of the South American mainland, inhabited by the Amerindians

1596 Visited by Captain Keymis of The Darling, reported as uninhabited
1628 Charles I grants Tobago to the Earl of Pembroke
1641 Charles I of England grants Tobago to the Duke of Courland (Modern Latvia)
1666 Courlanders leave
1762 Tobago captured by the British
1771 First slave uprising
1776 Oldest Forest Reserve in the Western Hemisphere designated in Tobago
1781 French capture Tobago
1793 British recapture Tobago
1801 Second slave uprising

1816 One company of Free Blacks from the US (mainly Baptists) settle in Tobago
1818 Methodist Mission established
1834 Emancipation Day, 1st August
1874 Old House of Assembly and Legislative Council replaced by single Legislative Council
1876 Belmanna Riots
1899 Tobago declared a Ward of the Colony of Trinidad and Tobago
1940 Crown Point Airport opens
1962 Trinidad and Tobago becomes an independent sovereign state
1963 Hurricane Flora devastates Tobago
1976 Trinidad and Tobago becomes a twin-island Republic with a President
1980 Tobago House of Assembly restored
2012 The Tobago House of Assembly confers for the first time its highest honour (the Tobago Medal of Honour) to three sons of the soil

SOME INTERESTING FACTS AND AMAZING FICTION

- Bloody Bay, on the Leeward coast, is named after a battle between English soldiers and slaves in 1771 that turned the blue waters red with blood. However, some claim the water was stained by red earth deposits.
- The 14,000-acre Central Forest Reserve, established by British colonial authorities on the 13th April 1776 "for the preservation of the rains", is the oldest protected rainforest in the Western Hemisphere.
- Man O'War Bay is reputed to be the site of buried pirate treasure.
- Thomas Aristis, renowned as one of the last British pirates, outmanoeuvred the Royal Navy and sought refuge in Pirates Bay in 1718. However, he was later murdered by one of his crew as he slept.
- The Easter Tuesday Buccoo Goat Races (a unique sport) were originally introduced by the Barbadian Samuel Callender in 1925.
- Richmond Great House, near Glamorgan on the Windward coast, was built in the 18th century and restored by Professor Hollis Lynch, who now runs it as a guest house and restaurant and home to his extensive collection of African art and textiles.
- Bacolet Bay Beach was the location for the 1960 movie, Swiss Family Robinson and a favourite frolicking spot for the Beatles in the late 1960s and early 1970s.
- Fisherman Brush, so the legend goes, was jailed ninety-nine times for stick fighting.

- Gang Gang Sara, the obeah woman of folklore, is believed to be buried in Golden Lane. She 'flew' from Africa to Les Coteaux searching for her family and found them in Golden Lane, where she also found and married her sweetheart Tom. When he died, she climbed a silk cotton tree ready for the return flight to Africa but found she'd lost the art of flight through eating salt.
- The mystery of African slave Betty Stiven's tomb in Plymouth (pictured) lies in the inscription: "What was remarkable about her; she was a mother without knowing it and a wife without letting her husband know it, except by her kind indulgences to him." Possible solutions are that 23 year-old Betty was the lover of wealthy Dutch planter Alex Stiven, who raised their child without recognising Betty as the mother; or that the relationship between Betty and Alex was kept secret and when she died in childbirth, Alex commemorated their passion with this cryptic message.
Photo: Oswin Browne

Tobago has gifted the world with many individuals who are recognised nationally and internationally as icons, exemplars and persons who have contributed to the island's reputation and development.

The island's highest accolade, The Tobago Medal of Honour, was awarded to:

Arthur Napoleon Raymond Robinson. He will always be remembered for the relentless struggle he waged for the establishment of the Tobago House of Assembly in 1980 and for the setting up of the International Criminal Court (ICC) in 2002. He is the only person to have held the country's three highest public offices - Chairman of the Tobago House of Assembly, Prime Minister and President of Trinidad and Tobago. The island's international Airport is named after him.

James Biggart, Tobago's First Member of the Legislative Council. Elected in 1925, he never failed to highlight Tobago's potential as a prime tourist resort and the urgency of better communications between Trinidad and Tobago. An agriculturalist, he was a constant advocate of Tobago's cocoa and animal production.

Alfonso Philbert James, better known as "Fargo", succeeded Biggart. A contractor and trade unionist, he represented Tobago in the legislative Council from 1946 to 1961 and fought relentlessly to improve the lives of his fellow countrymen.

Other notable individuals are:

The Right Rev Claude Berkley, the first person from Tobago to be enthroned as the Anglican Bishop of Trinidad and Tobago.

Dwight Eversley Yorke, Footballer Extraordinaire, from Canaan, represented Trinidad and Tobago 72 times and holds the record, with two other international players, of having participated in 6 different FIFA World Cup competitions. He captained the nation's Soca Warriors in all games during the FIFA World Cup in Germany, 2006.

Claude Noel, Professional Boxer from Roxborough, the nation's first boxing World Champion, held the WBA's World Lightweight title and the Commonwealth Lightweight title.

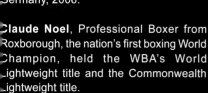

Calypso Rose, **McCartha Linda Sandy-Lewis**, is the Mother of Calypso. She wrote over 800 songs and recorded 20 albums that exemplified her fusion of the rhythms and melodies of Africa and the Caribbean. She won the coveted Calypso Queen title five times and is perhaps best remembered for the Calypso Anthem, Fire in Me Wire, and the Road March – Gimme More Tempto – the first woman to win this title in 1977.

Orthneil Bacchus, 'Tobago Crusoe', an Ambassador of Calypso and Ex-tempo in Europe. He performed with The Mighty Sparrow Youth Brigade Tent in Port of Spain for many years as both Calypsonian and MC. He won the Calypso Monarch crown in 1983 and is a major contributor to the promotion of Calypso in the United Kingdom.

Winston Bailey, 'The Mighty Shadow', though born in Trinidad, grew up in Les Coteaux in Tobago. He won the Road March in 1974 and in 2001 he won both the International Soca Monarch and the Road March titles. An accomplished performer with a distinctive style.

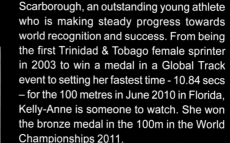

Kelly-Anne Kaylene Baptiste, from Scarborough, an outstanding young athlete who is making steady progress towards world recognition and success. From being the first Trinidad & Tobago female sprinter in 2003 to win a medal in a Global Track event to setting her fastest time - 10.84 secs – for the 100 metres in June 2010 in Florida, Kelly-Anne is someone to watch. She won the bronze medal in the 100m in the World Championships 2011.

John Arnold, composer, accompanist and arranger with an impressive and unrivalled record of promoting the culture of Tobago as an Events Manager of the island's signature events, practicing artist and officer in the Division of Tourism and Transportation, Tobago House of Assembly. John is the Founder and Musical Director of the illustrious Signal Hill Alumni Choir and leader of Tobago's only Jazz ensemble the Kariwak Players.

Carlton Robert Ruthven Ottey. Born in Scarborough in 1914, he was the Founder of the Trinidad & Tobago Arts Festival and the first Tobagonian to write a history of Tobago published in 1949.

Patrick Arnold, an outstanding record of services to the promotion of pan as Chair of PanTrinbago and current Chair of the National Carnival Commission.

Dodderidge H N Alleyne. Born in Charlotteville in 1927, Dodderidge is a graduate in Economics from Oxford who became the Head of The Public Service and Secretary to the Cabinet under Dr Eric Williams. From there, he became the Trinidad and Tobago Permanent Representative to the United Nations – the first Tobagonian to hold this position. He was awarded the Chaconia Medal (Gold) in 1986.

Senator Dr Eastlynne McKenzie. Born in 1941, she gained her doctorate in 1987 in Human Resource Development. In 1995, she became an independent Senator and to date (2012) she is the first and only Tobagonian to lead the Independent Senate Bench. She is a recognised advocate for challenged children and an ardent supporter and performer of the Arts.

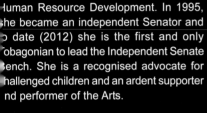

Rev Patricia Stephens, Author, Spiritual Mother and leading advocate for Spiritual Baptists in the United Kingdom.

Dr Edwin Wilberforce Carrington. Born in 1938 at Parlatuvier, he has an impressive record of public service – Chief of Economics & Statistics, CARICOM Secretariat; Director of Trade and Integration Division, CARICOM and High Commissioner to Guyana. In 1992, he was appointed Secretary-General of CARICOM and is the first citizen of Trinidad and Tobago to serve three terms as Secretary-General.

Josanne Lucas. The island's first female World Championship medalist in the 400m hurdles in 2009.

Eric Morton Roach. Eric was Tobago's first and only playwright to receive the nation's Humming Bird medal (Gold) for his work as a writer. In 1974, he was posthumously awarded First Place for Poetry and Playwriting in Jamaica.

Renny Quow. Another of the island's successful athletes, winning Tobago's first

Olive Theodore Sawyer. Consistent and unwavering commitment, spanning over forty years, to her community, particularly the less fortunate and challenged adults and children. Olive was the first Tobagonian appointed to the Independent Senate bench in 1981, serving until 1986.

Dr Jacob Delworth Elder. Affectionately known as JD Elder, he was the nation's leading authority on culture. He is best known for conceptualising the Tobago Heritage Festival and being instrumental in introducing the Best Village Competition. He was the Founding Director of the National Archives of Trinidad and Tobago.

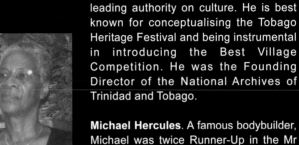

Michael Hercules. A famous bodybuilder, Michael was twice Runner-Up in the Mr Universe Competition and five times Mr West Indies before being inducted into the WITCO Sports Hall of Fame. In 1963, he joined the Prison Service rising to the rank of Commissioner of Prisons.

Duane Dove, Sommelier and pioneering eco-friendly cocoa farmer whose fine-flavoured cocoa is used to produce what international gourmands acknowledge as the finest chocolates in the world.

Pam Nicholson. 'Sister Pam' became the first female to win a seat in the General Elections in Tobago. She contested the elections three times and won her Tobago West seat on each occasion. She held ministerial positions in two administrations and was the first Tobago Woman to be appointed a Government Minister.

Victor Bruce. Victor has a number of distinguished 'firsts'. The first national to be appointed Governor of the country's Central Bank; the first Tobagonian to be awarded the Trinity Cross and the first Caribbean-born person to become Governor of the Central Bank of an African Country – Sierra Leone.

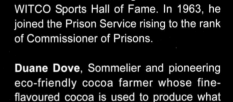

ANNUAL EVENTS

Tobago Festival
Tobago Fest, first held in 1998 and celebrated each September, includes a parade of bands, art, historical exhibitions and fetes. It opens with a Festival Queen Competition in Roxborough followed next morning by a J'Ouvert parade in the village of Plymouth, a parade of costumed bands on the streets of Scarborough and on the final day, a beach fete at Store Bay.

Spiritual (Shouter) Baptist Liberation Day
Spiritual Shouter Baptist is a unique religion specific to Trinidad comprising elements of both Protestant Christianity and African dogma and rituals. It is a dynamic and vibrant religion representing both the spontaneity and rhythms of Africa and the restrained, traditional tenets of Christianity. 30th March marks the repeal of the Shouter Prohibition Ordinance which banned the activities and observances of the religion.

The Tobago Culinary Festival
This free international event in May is aimed at showcasing the best of the world's cuisine with an emphasis on Tobago dishes. It is held at the Pigeon Point Heritage Park.

The Blue Food Festival
'Blue Food' covers all root crops found on the island. This Festival is in October at Bloody Bay, Tobago with a cooking competition to choose the most skilled chef using the root crop – Dasheen. There are usually other fringe events such as a Queen Show and cultural show.

Fashion Weekend
Caribbean followers of fashion congregate at The Pigeon Point beachfront in May to eyeball the creations of the region's designers and savour the trappings of the fashion world Tobago style.

Folk singers at the Heritage Festival. *Photo: Oswin Browne*

Jazz Experience
The Tobago Jazz Experience is a celebration of jazz and indigenous music of the Caribbean. Scheduled for April each year, the visitor will not only experience the music but able to savour and participate in the cultural and historical practices that define Tobago as an ideal destination.

Heritage Festival
The largest and most renowned of all Tobago's Festivals, 'Heritage' is a multi-event showcase of Tobago's dance, music, religion, rituals and cuisine. The Festival is staged at several villages with each village having its own signature event. The most celebrated of this is the village of Moriah's Ole Time Wedding.

Harvest & Fisherman's Festivals
Always on a Sunday, these festivals are held in villages all over the island. Harvests were a thanksgiving celebration by farmers. The Fisherman's festivals are usually in coastal villages, mainly on St Peter's Day (29 June).

Underwater Carnival
In July at Pigeon Point.

Emancipation Day Heritage Parade
A parade commemorating Emancipation Day on the 1st of August from Bon Accord to Pigeon Point.

Pirogue Festival
A fun day for the whole family with boat races, music and food at Man O'War Bay in Charlotteville in November.

Carnival
Not on the grand scale as Trinidad but Tobago's celebrations begin soon after Christmas with several events culminating in a number of traditional events – the Steel Band competition (Panorama) and Queen and Calypso Shows – and the street processions of masqueraders and musicians on Carnival Monday and Tuesday in February or March.

Muhtadi International Drumming Festival
A rhythmic feast featuring drummers and percussionists from all over the world. Each August since 2005, this Festival has grown into a major international platform of the most skilled drummers with workshops and live performances over two days.

Assembly Day
The Tobago House of Assembly celebrates and recognises Tobagonians with an award for their achievements. Usually in December with exhibitions, sports and fun activities.

Trinidad and Tobago's very own 3 Canal performing at Tobago Jazz Experience. *Photo: Oswin Browne*

Bon Accord Lagoon
Photo: Oswin Browne

PLACES OF INTEREST

Crown Point
Kariwak Wellness Centre: located in the Kariwak
Village Hotel. Offers holistic health facilities,
yoga, and meditation in a beautiful garden setting

Store Bay
Fort Milford: sunset-viewing vantage spot, built by
the British in 1777

Pigeon Point
Pigeon Point Heritage Park: Tobago's iconic
beach, with water sports facilities and trips to
Buccoo Reef and Nylon Pool

Scarborough, the capital of Tobago
Fort King George: the island's main fortification
built by the British in 1804. Besides cemetery,
chapel and cells, the Tobago Museum is also
housed here in the former barracks.
Botanic Gardens: close to highway with fine
collection of cultivated plants that grow wild
throughout the island.

Plymouth
Fort James: built by the British in 1768 and
named after King James II.
Courlander Monument represents 'Freedom' and
was unveiled in 1976 in memory of the original
Latvian settlers.
Mystery Tombstone: erected in memory to Betty
Stiven in 1783.

Galleries & Museums
Art Gallery, Lowlands
Dillon's Art Studio & Gallery
Dive Museum, Bacolet
Fort King George, Scarborough

Casinos
Royalton, Crown Point
Sunset Palm, Buccoo Junction
Jade Monkey, Fortune Plaza, Milford Road

Windward Coast
Pembroke Heritage Village: new facility for
heritage and community events
Richmond Great House, the oldest Great House
built on a sugar plantation in 1776 with an
extensive collection of African Art.
Argyle Falls, a three tiered waterfall.
Tobago Cocoa Estate, Roxborough: working
cocoa estate and heritage park
Flagstaff Hill, the site of an American Military
lookout and Radio Tower during World War II

Leeward Coast

Cuffie River Nature Retreat: ideal for birdwatching, tours

Adventure Park & Nature Reserve, a 12-acre organic estate with a butterfly garden and shelter for endangered species.

Sugar factory built by Courlanders in 1670 on the Franklyn Estate near Arnos Vale with a water-driven wheel and steam boiler.

Main Ridge & Forest Reserve. The island's celebrated reserve, the oldest in the western hemisphere.

BEACHES

No other Caribbean island can boast to offer the discerning visitor the same range of largely deserted beaches, varying from the pristine white coral sands of the Caribbean coast to the dark volcanic sands of the Atlantic coast.

Please keep in mind that nude and/or topless sunbathing is illegal in Tobago. This practice is often considered highly offensive to the local population. Please also remember to cover-up when leaving the beach.

Besides the most popular and photographed Pigeon Point and the equally accessible Store Bay, both close to the airport there are a number of other stunning beaches including:

Back Bay: isolated, accessed by trail between Mt Irvine and Grafton

Buccoo: narrow beach at heart of famous goat and crab racing venue

Canoe Bay: a short drive off Milford Road. Calm water and beach bar

Leeward Coast

Mt Irvine: favourite with surfers

Great Courland Bay: famous for nesting leatherback turtles

Castara: another secluded masterpiece in fishing community, with restaurants and bar

Englishman's Bay: Off main road, a secret worth discovering. Ideal for snorkelling

Parlatuvier: another secluded fishing village site

Bloody Bay: its peaceful ambience belies a bloody past, site of battle between British and Amerindians

Man O'War Bay: Charlotteville's showpiece

Windward Coast

Bacolet: location for the 1960 film, Swiss Family Robinson

Bellevue: rare calm waters

Granby Point: dark sand

Little Rockly Bay: for Atlantic breakers

King's Bay: long stretch with calm waters and good facilities.

Speyside: within swimming/snorkelling distance of coral reefs

Itsy-Bitsy Playhouse: It is not the normal theatre but one which offers its patrons local food, exhibition of artefacts and total all-local Tobago culture all-year round. Be awed by the flaming limbo, traditional folk songs, drumology and the talents of many local artistes.

A moment's relaxation at Pigeon Point
Photo: Ian Brierley

Tobago beckons you

The warmth and culture of Tobago reads like a wish list for naturalists, beach lovers, historians and cultural enthusiasts. The smiling faces of 54,000 Tobagonians, countless beaches and cultural events and more than 32 battles mix with 220 species of birds, 17 bats, 5 marine turtles, 16 lizards, 14 frogs, 24 non-poisonous snakes and 12 mammals on this 300 square kilometre land mass.

Tobago boasts of changing hands more often than any other Caribbean island. This spec of lush green land bounced between the Dutch, the Courlanders, the Spanish, the British and later the French. Anchored by the rich roots of its African heritage, with the flamboyant influence of its sister island Trinidad, Tobago continues to inspire the passions of visitors and locals alike.

Tobago's colourful heritage is nestled into every corner of the island, in the names of places such as L'Anse Fourmi from its French roots and Charlotteville from the British. Villages like Castara and Buccoo tell tales of the long lost Amerindian presence, while Bloody Bay and Pirates Bay seduce the imagination with rumours of undiscovered buried treasure and bloody battles. These tranquil blue bays, with their high cliffs, cascading greenery and fringing reefs are home to more romantic stories today.

The south-western end provides sun-drenched beaches and all the modern conveniences of hotels, great restaurants and lively entertainment. Journeying northwards, towns give way to sleepy fishing villages in steep valleys shaded by the umbrella of the Main Ridge Forest Reserve, the oldest in the Western Hemisphere. The heart of these communities beats to the rhythms of the land and the sea. Artisanal fishing and fresh herbs from tiny home gardens fill pots that bubble with flavourful local dishes.

Villages such as Castara and Parlatuvier lure visitors with the drifting scent of fresh bread baking in traditional outdoor dirt ovens. In Roxborough, Tobago's world-renowned cocoa is once-again delighting chocolate-lovers. Parlatuvier boasts traditionally preserved sun-dried, smoked corned fish.

Accommodation is as diverse as its landscape – large hotels, impressive colonial-style villas overlooking isolated bays and quaint apartments and homestays that give a glimpse into Tobago life.

Come to Tobago and learn why 54,000 people are smiling.

Dr Adana N. Mahase-Gibson

Leather craft shop-holder in Scarborough
Photo: Ian Brierley

Tobagonian football legend, Dwight Yorke, right, takes in a round of golf. *Photo: Oswin Browne*

A warm Tobago welcome
Photo: Stephen Broadbridge

Carnival revellers
Photo: Oswin Browne

Selling local crafts at Store Bay
Photo: Stephen Broadbridge

A chance meeting
Photo: Stephen Broadbridge

Waiting for school to finish in Parlatuvier
Photo: Stephen Broadbridge

The idyllic Tobago lifestyle

To say that the Tobago lifestyle is a relaxed one is a gross understatement. Trinidad is relaxed. Tobago is on pause. . . a deliciously divine, continuous recess from life's hustle and bustle. In Tobago, life is laid back and never in a rush to get away. Everyone is always taking a breather, stopping to smell the sea breeze and taking a dip in the warm tropical waters. It is a lifestyle to be envied, so much so that many foreigners have made Tobago their permanent abode in order to live in paradise. For those born and bred on the island, Tobago is simply home.

PEOPLE

There's a longstanding joke that everyone in Tobago is related. It is truly a tribute to the strong family and community ties that bind Tobagonians. While there are significant percentages of foreigners and Trinidadians who live on the island, the native Tobagonian contingent remains strong, thus preserving and propagating the island values and vibes.

WORK

Tobago's economy revolves around the tourism and hospitality industry. As such, this is the largest employer on the island. Many people work in hotels and guesthouses, restaurants and other food places, tourism activity centres and support services, tourism-associated organisations, and the like.

The fishing industry is another important employer, with fishermen being the primary bread winners in many Tobago villages. The Castara Fisherman's Fête, Charlotteville Fisherman's Fest and St. Peter's Day Fisherman's Festival recognise their hard work and contribution to the culture and character of the island.

PLAY

In Tobago, every day is a day at the beach… literally. No one lives too far away from the sea, and as such, Tobagonians live their lives by the ebb and flow of the water.

While the island has produced outstanding athletes like international football star Dwight Yorke, it is a more unconventional sport that is a favourite amongst Tobagonians – goat racing. It is so celebrated that there is an annual festival – the Buccoo Goat Race Festival, which began in 1925. The event attracts thousands of spectators from all over the world.

Apart from being home to many events and festivals, Tobago has a growing nightlife culture, with an increasingly active restaurant and party scene. Although there are many modern, "new school" forms of entertainment, the most popular event in Tobago is one that has been around for decades. It's called Sunday School, which is a street or block party where locals come together for food, live entertainment – in the form of steel pan and a rhythm section, and a really great time.

WORSHIP

Tobagonians' lifestyle being steeped in traditional values and the teachings of our ancestors. The belief in and use of "bush" medicine – teas, ointments, even baths – is still commonplace, even amongst the younger generations. While all major religions are represented on the island, the Spiritual Baptist faith is the strongest. Fervent followers can be seen on a daily basis, preaching, singing praise songs and dancing (aka catching power) in various public spaces.

Sonja Sinaswee

Boat repairs at Charlottville
Photo: Ian Brierley

Hauling the catch
Photo: Oswin Browne

A walk through the forest to Pirates Bay
Photo: Stephen Broadbridge

A nirvana for naturalists

It is neither an idle boast nor a marketing hype to claim that Tobago is the premiere eco-tourism destination in the world and is truly a nirvana for naturalists.

This little island nirvana is renowned for:

- Diverse South American flora and fauna
- The oldest legally protected rainforest in the Western World
- Secluded waterfalls alive to the 220 species of birds and tropical rainforest life
- Windswept cliffs that have become nesting grounds of seabird colonies
- Stunning Coral reefs with 44 coral species encircling the island, and
- Endangered giant leatherback turtles and other marine turtles that nest on the beaches.

Rainforests are universally recognised as the most biologically diverse eco-systems and has become an all-embracing term synonymous with sustainability, protection and the 'grandeur of the green'. For naturalists there are rainforests of the land and of the sea.

Tobago offers you these two rainforests – the Rainforest of the Land and the Rainforest of the Sea.

THE RAINFOREST OF THE LAND

Having been part of South America, Tobago shares the range of this area's rainforest biodiversity and even shares some species with northern Venezuela that do not exist in Trinidad. It is this diversity that sets Tobago's Rainforest of the Land apart from all others in the Caribbean, save Trinidad. And the beauty is that they are all easily accessible to be seen and observed within the confines of this small island.

The main area is the Main Ridge Forest Reserve; the oldest protected rainforest that is home to most of the

White plumeria
Photo: Oswin Browne

Views around Charlotteville
Photo: Kyle Walcott

The spectacular heliconia
Photo: Oswin Browne

Clockwise from top left – Hibiscus. *Photo: Oswin Browne*; One of the island's many rainforest flowers. *Photo: Stephen Broadbridge*; Wattled jacana. *Photo: Oswin Browne*; Orange-winged Amazon parrot. *Photo: Ryan P. Mannette*

...sland's species of vibrantly hued forest birds including: the Tobago Blue-backed Manakin, the White-tailed Sabrewing Humming Bird, the Blue-crowned Motmot, the Rufus-tailed Jacamar, the Yellow-legged Thrush, the Olivaceous Woodcreeper, the Collared Trogon and many more.

RAINFOREST WILDLIFE

Over 220 species of birds have been recorded in Tobago of which about 100 can be spotted in the Main Ridge Forest Reserve together with mammalian wildlife such as armadillos, agoutis, wild hogs, red squirrels, raccoons and opossums.

Several bat species, including a piscivorous (fish-eating) bat also inhabits the forest. The Reserve is also home to a number of non-venomous snakes as well as lizards and frogs.

Plant and insect life has been poorly recorded and provide a real challenge for anyone wanting to discover new species or simply record what exists.

RAINFOREST VEGETATION

The Main Ridge Reserve offers the opportunity to examine the multi-dimensional strata of a tropical rainforest. A closed 30 – 50 metres (10 – 165 feet) high canopy umbrellas the rainforest with ferns, palms and slow-growing trees, all o... which do not need much light, dominating the understory.

On the ground layer, there is a profusion of seedlings and herbaceous plants as well as a plethora of wild orchids, bromeliads and other epiphytes. Rippling streams and cascading waterfalls add a refreshing dimension to this wonderful reserve.

RAINFOREST REGENERATION

In 1963, Hurricane Flora, with her terrible winds and destructive rainfall, ravaged about 75% of the forests in Tobago. Four decades later, Tobago's rainforest is a living example of a rainforest regenerating as lush ground vegetation and slender trees emerge in a protected environment. This form of conservation is indeed very rare...

Small Fall in Charlotteville
Photo: Kyle Walcott

Copper-rumped hummingbird
Photo: Oswin Browne

Clockwise from top left – Tropical kingbird. *Photo: Ryan P. Mannette*; Bananaquit. *Photo: Oswin Browne*; Barred antshrike *Photo: Oswin Browne*; Rufous-breasted wren. *Photo: Oswin Browne*

BIRD WATCHING

From Tanagers to Mockingbirds, Hummingbirds to Woodpeckers, there's almost nowhere in this unspoilt, verdant isle that isn't a birdwatcher's paradise. Such is Tobago's natural attraction to avifauna, over 210 species of birds have been spotted.

Positioned so close to Venezuela, Tobago is an ideal stopover point for migratory birds. Some northern birds either stay in Tobago during winter or pass through on their way south. Conversely, during the sub-equatorial winter months, some southern species from as far as Argentina regularly visit Tobago.

Seabirds also occupy a special place for Tobago birdwatchers with two islands off the coast – Little Tobago and St Giles Island – renowned for their seabird colonies.

Up to 58 species have been recorded on Little Tobago, 33 of them breeding. Species native to the island include the Red-footed Booby and Brown Booby and among its migrant seabirds are the Red-tailed Tropicbird, Brown Noddy, Sooty

Tern, Bridled Tern, Roseate Tern and Laughing Gulls.

St Giles Island supports one of the region's most important large seabird breeding colonies in its 72 acres. Magnificent Frigatebirds, the Red-footed Booby, Red-billed Tropicbirds, Audubon's Shearwater, Noddy Terns and Brown Boobies have all been sighted on this island.

Other birdwatching sites can be found at Store Bay, Buccoo, Mount Irvine, Plymouth, Hillsborough Dam, Grafton Caledonia Bird & Wildlife Sanctuary, Adventure Farm and Nature Reserve and the Cuffie River Nature Retreat.

RAINFORESTS OF THE SEA

There are entire sections of the island of Tobago that have gone virtually unchanged and would be easily recognisable to the ancient mariners that first set foot on this verdant isle.

In Tobago's Rainforest of the Seas, the Guyana Current flows over the healthy, robust reefs, feeding and nourishing a

Purpose-built walkway through Fifi Estate in Bon Accord
Photo: Stephen Broadbridge

This idyllic vista reflects two of Tobago's main
assets – beautiful beaches and lush rainforests
Photo: Stephen Broadbridge

The stunning blue crowned motmot
Photo: Ryan P. Mannette

A leatherback turtle creates a burrow in which
to lay her eggs before returning to the sea
Photo: Oswin Browne

Clockwise from top left – Anolis lizard. *Photo: Ryan P. Mannette*; The waters are home to a spectacular array of marine life. *Photo courtesy Tourism Development Company*; French grunt. *Photo: Ryan P. Mannette*; Green iguana. *Photo: Stephen Broadbridge*

marine eco-system of giants. In this nutrient rich environment, there are massive hard corals, including the world's largest brain coral and fields of huge barrel sponges twisted and sculpted by the constant press of moving water.

From big, in-your-face experiences to hidden macro kingdoms, you will find something in the island's Rainforest of the Sea to excite you. There are numerous dive sites to guarantee signature experiences as no two dives will ever be alike in Tobago.

Foremost among these is Tobago's Buccoo Reef Marine Park, rated as the third most spectacular reef in the world by Oceanographer Jacques Cousteau. The Reef's features are:

- The Reef Flats – Five reef flats with a fascinating and diverse array of aquatic life that enclose a shallow reef lagoon dominated by Staghorn and Star corals.

- The Bon Accord Lagoon – Fringed by red mangrove wetlands and dominated by microalgae and beds of seagrass

- The Fore-Reef – Slopes to depths from 15 to 30 metres and offers excellent views of Brain, Star and Elkhorn corals

- The Nylon Pool – A shallow, pure white sand area with crystal clear and rejuvenating waters.

TURTLE WATCHING

Tobago is one of the few places still privileged to be a leatherback maternity home and hatching nursery. Other species such as the green and hawksbill turtles also nest in Tobago. Turtles require soft, dry sand to nest and lay in the greatest density on the expanse of beach between Turtle Beach Hotel and the Black Rock Rover.

You can watch these magnificent creatures hatch their eggs at the Grafton Beach, Stonehaven Beach and the Great Courland Bay. The egg-laying season is between March & July and The Trinidad & Tobago Field Naturalists Club organises nightly trips to the beach during the season.

Leatherback turtle hatchling making its way to the sea
Photo: Ryan P. Mannette

Heritage Festival opening
night performance
Photo: Oswin Browne

O n this tiny island the 18th century collides with the 21st: internet resort bookings and helicopter tours versus African ancestor worship and folktales. Modern traditions, like Buccoo's 'Sunday School' street party with steelband and DJs co-exist with revived customs like the Old Time Wedding, a prominent feature of July's Heritage Festival.

One custom which you're likely to come across is 'pulling seine': the communal retrieving of fishing nets cast close to shore. Once they've spotted shoals of small fish like sprats, jacks or even larger bonito, fishermen in boats drop the net in a circle from the shore. Any and everybody can help to pull in the catch, part of which they can claim as payment for their effort. This is both practical and

part of the 'Len han' tradition common throughout the Caribbean: the co-operative work ethic of African villages, which the slaves brought with them and put to good use after Emancipation: building houses or boats, clearing land for cultivation, planting and harvesting.

Many of Tobago's older traditions were saved for posterity thanks to the late JD Elder, a noted anthropologist/ ethnomusicologist, who insisted they were incorporated in the Heritage Festival, when it was established in the 1980s.

The common feature of these older traditions is the mixing of African and European styles and customs. Among the core events which are staged in authentic village settings are the Moriah Wedding with its groom in stove pipe and tail coat,

Moriah Ole Time Wedding
Photo: Oswin Browne

Moriah Ole Time Wedding street parade
Photo: Oswin Browne

Traditional dress and dance
during the Heritage Festival
Photo: Oswin Browne

pride with trousseau on head, the procession accompanied by fiddler and tambrin drummers. Here the costuming may be European but the music moves to distinctly African rhythms.

Plymouth stages an old time carnival with African stickfighting and masquerade characters with English titles like Duke, Valentine, Show Boy and Commander who parade and dance in decorated European top hats, but whose origins lie in the street festivals of Nigeria. They are joined by Ju Ju warriors, Jab Jabs and devils dressed in satin, reminiscent of old English clowns.

Bethel and Plymouth are also home to famous Speech bands, an entirely unique Tobago tradition linked to carnival. A cast of costumed characters including Creator, Sealey, The King, Hero Conqueror, The Duke of Wellington, The Doctor, My Boy Pompey speechify in rhyme, a form

but which obviously owes much to the vibrant African oral tradition.

The Heritage Festival's Folk Fiesta showcases dancing, singing and drumming and a tambrin band competition. Tobagonian music and dance is quite distinct from that of its larger sister island. While some Creole dances like the Belé and Piqué are found in both islands, the Reel and Jig and the accompanying tambrin music are uniquely Tobagonian.

Tambrin (from tambourine) is quintessential Tobago music. It is driven by three shallow goatskin 'tambrin' drums: the cutter (high pitch), roller (rhythm) and boom (bass). The drums provide an African basis for the lead instrument the fiddle and the added percussion of a steel triangle.

Tambrin bands dominated village social events (processions, weddings, boat christenings, harvest festivals) and island

'Dancing the cocoa' is part of
the Heritage Festival
Photo: Oswin Browne

Traditional log-sawing is part
of the Heritage Festival
Photo: Oswin Browne

Tamboo Bamboo Carnival. *Photo: Oswin Browne*

Tambrin was traditionally used for both adapted European dances like the quadrille, polka, waltz, Lancers and the South American pasea and for the African derived ritual dances-the Reel and Jig. These last two dances are evidence traditions which survived colonial oppression by camouflaging themselves in the European form of British sailors' dances.

The Reel, Jig, Saraka from Pembroke and even the Belé are dances invoking the spirits of the ancestors and dead, a tactic for survival, inspiration and resistance since slavery days. As the dance progressed spirits would manifest themselves 'riding' or possessing dancers through whom they revealed messages, suppressed information or the cause of sickness, entrapment or other problems. The Reel was danced on many occasions-at the annual wake for the dead, a boat launching or seine hanging, during times of sickness or recovery, evil or hardship and on bachelor's night before a wedding

African influences survive in other traditions: folklore, agricultural superstitions and bush medicine. There are the tales of Wawa Douglas and Conga Brown who when beaten by the slave master, magically transferred the lashes to the planter's wife and Congo Ellis who because he didn't eat salt was able to fly back to Africa.

While gardeners wouldn't dream of planting if a funeral was taking place in the village, they would make sure to bathe before entering a yam plot as these tubers are regarded as particularly sensitive. Folk cures include matte root for diabetes and snake bites; bamboo lea for fevers, pneumonia or strokes and lizard grass for gastroenteritis.

Simon Lee

The Tobago tambrin has been something of a mystery to all who visit the island and even locals alike. The one common factor is that all admire the players of this simple drum and marvel at the type of music that comes from it. The point is that there is a lot to be learned from the people who play this instrument and from the music it produces. What really is this Tobago tambrin?

The tambrin is a type of drum that was discovered and developed by Tobagonians to satisfy the need to drum; a need that was suppressed by European colonisers during the period of the enslavement of the Africans. The tambrin first showed up in the west when the Europeans were engaged in their efforts to convert the Africans to Christianity. These missionaries shook their tambourine and banged its skin against the palm of the hand in order to produce the rhythms that accompanied their songs. This obviously gave the Africans ideas because when cheese was imported in circular boxes that were some four inches deep and about twelve to fourteen inches in diameter, the rims of these boxes were fitted with skins and played in a way that eventually led to the development of the phenomenon that we call the "Tobago tambrin". The name 'tambrin' really comes from tambourine.

As time passed, the Africans learned to make these drums better and to combine them in ways that created an orchestra. As with all African drum orchestras, a typical tambrin band comprises of a 'boom' (bass), a 'fuller' (mid range) and a 'cutter' which provides the high end of the music. To complete the orchestration a violin is used to play the tunes and a steel triangle for added rhythm.

The tambrin band became a feature of Tobago's folk music in the period following emancipation and has lasted to today. The band played music for wedding dances, bachelor's nights, wedding marches, socials and accompanied another Tobago folk creation called the Speech Band. Many locals will say however, that its most important function was within the ritual called the Reel Dance; a type of spiritual ritual that was conducted in order to communicate with the spirits of ancestors and seek their help in problem solving.

Today, much of this spirituality seems to have been lost but the instrument remains an integral part of the island's folk tradition and is largely featured in the annual Tobago Heritage Festival.

Photo: Oswin Browne
Words: Rawle Winston Titus

Steel band in full flow
Photo: Oswin Browne

'Round the neck' steelband
Photo: Oswin Browne

Tobago's home for the Arts

The Shaw Park Cultural Centre (SPCC) is the latest addition to Tobago's theatre land offering a smorgasbord of year-round activities.

Host of one of the region's renowned jazz festival, Tobago has long held its traditions in folklore and the arts and culture in an esteemed place, giving edificial energies to its heritage which has given the island well-regarded status regionally and on the international circuit.

Recognising that arts and culture are instrumental in helping to "attract young, educated professionals who will bring intellect, energy and talent to the area", the Tobago House of Assembly is constructing a modern 5,000-seat centre for the arts, with theatre and conferencing facilities for events accommodating in excess of 100 patrons.

The Centre, situated in Scarborough, is a multifunctional facility catering to the needs of Tobagonians and also to local, regional and international event promoters. It will serve as a permanent fixture on the Trinidad and Tobago performing arts landscape providing an extraordinary experience for audiences.

A contemporary arts centre with a social and education mission, the SPCC will play host to a lineup of local, national and international arts programming including events such as gospel festivals, comedy shows, jazz festival, school music and drama competitions and Carnival activities. It will offer also limited use for major sporting activities.

Future programming will include Tobago's annual Heritage Festival, jazz, dance, and classical concerts, appearances by world-famous performers, as well as a variety of plays and musicals, intimate cabaret performances, appearances by local and regional thespians and a multitude of other unique entertainment options.

The Tobago Heritage Library, which will be housed here and open to the public, with significant music, posters, recordings and other artifacts on Tobago, will act as a museum and education centre. Large and small spacious rooms that can be utilised for training facilities are also available for rental.

This multi million project showcases a building with a fan-shaped footprint with seating for 5,000 with the ability to allow for small performance seating of 1,200 in the main auditorium. This performance area carries a modular stage, which would allow for the parade of Carnival Bands and steelband Panorama activities. Green room and dressing room facilities are provided along with rehearsal rooms in the backstage area.

SPCC invites promoters to explore the space and, to vacationers, when you are planning your trip to Tobago, include, among the nightlife activities, some theatre.

Caroline Ravello has a Masters in Communications and is experienced in journalism and communication

The annual Easter Goat Race
Photo: Oswin Browne

BUCCOO INTEGRATED FACILITY

Rural and Community tourism is becoming increasingly important to Tobago's Tourism and by extension the overall economy and the Tobago tourism product. The importance of tourism to local economies differs across the world. Some places, like major cities, have large investments in the tourism industry, while rural areas may lag behind. In Tobago, we are mindful that all the communities play an integral part in the development of Tourism on the Island.

Visitors all across the globe are seeking new experiences and Buccoo provides us with an opportunity to develop a facility which offers a unique experience. As visitors to Tobago search out new destinations and experiences, rural tourism (if organised and marketed properly) can provide a unique opportunity to fulfil visitors' needs. Buccoo is well known for the weekly street party aptly dubbed "Sunday School", the Buccoo Reef and the annual Easter Goat Races.

Some of the rural areas in Tobago are a rich (often untapped) source of cultural and heritage tourism. Research in tourism has

shown repeatedly that a majority of travellers do participate in cultural and heritage tourism on their trips.

Buccoo Integrated facility provides us with the ideal opportunity to develop core activities in Buccoo that would provide locals and visitors an experience of a lifetime and certainly an appreciation of our cultural-heritage Tourism.

The facility provides the following:

- INFORMATION BOOTH – this is managed by a well trained and courteous staff. The booth would provide collateral material on places of interest in Tobago and offer some merchandise for sale to visitors.
- CRAFT BOOTHS – these booths would offer a variety of creative works in art and craft. These would range from batik, shell, leather, beads and other myriad creations as vendors provide the opportunity for custom made designs for visitors.
- RESTAURANT AND BAR – This area provides great ambience

as it is situated in an area overlooking the beach. Tobago is well known for its gastronomic festivals which features a lot of culinary creations. Some of the indigenous culinary offerings would be sold at this restaurant. Local entertainment would also be a feature of the restaurant.
- GOAT RACE FACILITY – This facility would be the Mecca of not only goat racing meets, but also provide a venue for other activities which includes concerts, movie presentations, children's activities, sports, trade exhibitions, folk theatre and many other events.
- MUSEUM – the Buccoo Museum would be a place to visit as persons would experience video presentations, pictorial presentations and other artefacts showcasing the history of the buccoo reef trade and goat racing. Visitors would also have the opportunity to purchase some memorabilia about Tobago.

John Arnold, Events Co-ordinator at the Division of Tourism and Transportation, Tobago House of Assembly

Joicie's

Try Bake ~~ **Salt Fish** ~~ **Shark** }} **Chicken Pelau**

Combo) Rice, Macaroni Pie, or Callaloo with Lentil Chicken, Pork or Fish

Coo-Coo, Callaloo or Lentil with Chicken, Pork or Fish

Coo-Coo, Provision, Dumplin, Lentil or Callaloo with Chicken Pork or Fish

Crab, Dumplin // Provision

Joicie's menu board reflects
the unique dishes of Tobago
Photo: Stephen Broadbridge

A feast of gastronomic delights

The island of curried crab and dumpling, Tobago is as much loved for its culinary offerings as it is for its natural beauty and charm. Casual and fine dining restaurants, takeaway joints, international fast food outlets and street vendors cater to the variety of tastes, which range from good home cooking to gourmet cuisine.

Over the years, Tobago has become as much a foodie paradise as a sun, sea and sand destination. Award-winning restaurants and delightful gourmet eateries are to be found throughout the island, although the majority are particularly concentrated on its western and southern ends in Crown Point, Mt. Pleasant, Buccoo to Plymouth and in Scarborough. They serve Asian, European (particularly Italian), American and Caribbean dishes. Fusion food is also on the rise.

Many restaurants and casual dining spots take advantage of Tobago's beautiful scenery. Most are open-air, bathing diners in the glorious Caribbean sun and seducing them with the relaxing sea breeze. Some are set in landscaped gardens, in the remains of old colonial plantation houses, or have breathtaking views of the ocean. Others are beautifully converted houses with indoor dining as well as outdoor seating on galleries and verandas.

Domestic and international tourism drive the food industry, so quite often the fine dining haunts open only for dinner, while the casual restaurants and takeaway outlets offer two or three meals a day. Whatever the meal, though, fresh seafood is a speciality. After all, the sea is but a walk or short drive away. Freshly caught fish, conch, crab, shrimp and lobster, especially prepared Creole style, are menu standouts and must haves.

In 1974, in his classic calypso and Road March winner, Bassman, the Mighty Shadow sang, "Ah was planning to forget calypso; and go and plant peas in Tobago". This line, which many young artistes have reworked and paid homage to in their own compositions, speaks

The popular Fish Pot restaurant is open "any time, any day"
Photo: Stephen Broadbridge

Preparing the popular
local dish, coo coo
Photo: Oswin Browne

Traditional dirt oven
Photo: Oswin Browne

directly to the lifestyle in Shadow's home; the calypso master is Les Couteaux-bred.

Traditionally, every Tobago family had a home garden, where three crops were a surety: pigeon peas, corn and ground provisions, in particularly dasheen. Hence, the popularity of three classic dishes: pigeon peas stewed in coconut milk, paimee (cornmeal dough filled with raisins, sugar and coconut), and blue boiled ground provisions or blue food.

Overall, the island's traditional cuisine is based on ground provisions and fresh fish, flavoured with plenty of herbs and seasonings. For the visitor, Store Bay is the destination for traditional Tobago food.

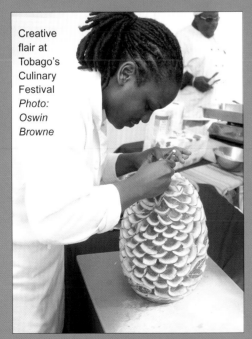

Creative flair at Tobago's Culinary Festival
Photo: Oswin Browne

Stalls line the open-air food court, serving up generous portions of blue food, callaloo, hearty soups, stewed and curried meats and seafood, and stewed peas and beans. After-meal indulgence calls for the island's famous sweets, including benne balls, guava cheese, pawpaw balls, sugar cake, tamarind balls and toolum.

Community harvests are an integral part of the local culinary traditions. Every year, villages around Tobago host a harvest, where residents get together to cook signature local dishes and share with one another and visitors. It is not a commercial endeavour, but an opportunity for villagers to celebrate the food of their area and to build community spirit. Larger harvests boast street parties, live entertainment and attract large visitor audiences.

Tobago's Blue Food Festival is the island's largest food event. Held annually in October at the Bloody Bay/L'Anse Fourmi recreation ground, the festival focuses on indigenous and creative food offerings. The star is dasheen, known internationally as taro and locally as blue food, so dubbed because some varieties of the root vegetable turn varying shades of blue and indigo when cooked. Every year, local cooks will vie for prizes in the Blue Food Cooking Competition and showcase their creativity in designing and producing dishes using dasheen.

Sonja Sinaswee

World class Tobago chocolates

Trinidad and Tobago is unique in the world of cocoa. Historically it is regarded as the "birthplace" of the Trinitario (native of Trinidad) germplasm and cocoa has been an important agricultural commodity for this country since the 19th century. In 1921, production peaked at over 30 million kilograms and Trinidad and Tobago was ranked in the top five global producers of cocoa. Tobago has made significant contributions to Trinidad and Tobago's production up until the early sixties when the Island was hit by hurricane Flora.

Trinidad and Tobago cocoa is unrivalled for its pleasant floral scent and unique taste. It is the essential ingredient in the chocolates of three of the nation's most renowned and internationally acclaimed chocolate makers – Isabel Brash, Gina Sonia Hardy and Duane Dove.

Tobagonian-born Duane Dove grew up on the island of Tobago. His parentage is both French and English. His ancestry goes all the way back to Scotland where his great great grandfather was born. He spent a larger part of his childhood helping out on the family's cocoa estate which involved harvesting, fermenting, sun drying cocoa beans and grading them.

In May 2005 he decided to begin the long journey of rejuvenating Tobago's once vibrant and productive cocoa industry. He sought the assistance of the best "cocoa minds" in Trinidad and Tobago which included the Cocoa Research Unit (CRU) of the University of Trinidad and Tobago, Centeno Government Cocoa Unit and the Cocoa & Coffee Board of Trinidad & Tobago, along with his committed staff. The estate, The Tobago Cocoa Estate, comprises of 47 acres (23.5 hectares) with the major crop being cocoa accompanied by other crops such as bananas, coffee, cassava, guava, papaya and a mix of exotic fruit trees. It is now a fully established cocoa estate growing some of the finest Trinitario strains, but, also a successful Agro-Tourism project offering estate tours with lunch and dinner included.

After seven years of intense planting and cultivation of the old Roxborough Cocoa Estate, Tobago Cocoa Estate is now into its 3rd harvest and for the very first time in 2011 produced two

separate batches of chocolates from the finest trinitario cocoa grown in Trinidad and Tobago!

The estate located in the district of Roxborough comprises 25 planted acres with an additional 22 acres to cultivate. Tobago Cocoa Estate made history on 12th January 2010 by producing Tobago's first and only Single Estate Chocolate bar. These are chocolates made solely with cocoa sourced at a Single farm. This model raises the bar and offers transparency and traceability and responsibility to the environment.

Today, Tobago Cocoa Estate W.I. Ltd is the only established estate on the island committed to bringing back cocoa production. Tobago Cocoa, as one of the island's main agricultural exports, has a significant international competitive advantage in terms of product quality, price and reputation. The estate is the only one of its kind with an agro-tourism link. During the years the estate has won several competitions for "Best Tree Crop" and "Integrated Farming".

In July 2011 Tobago Estate Chocolate was awarded the prestigious Great Taste Gold Star award from the London Guild of Fine Foods for its outstanding taste and quality. This was the first time ever a product of Trinidad and Tobago origin received such an award.

Tobago Estate Chocolate line includes 5 gram squares, 50 gram bars, 100 gram bars and 1000 gram coverture (blocks).

Its products are sold in selected shops in several countries – England, France, Germany, Switzerland, Holland, Trinidad and Tobago and throughout Scandinavia including 30 shops across Sweden. The chocolates are made in France by renowned Chocolatier Francois Pralus.

So when in Tobago, do not miss the chance to savour a chocolate of outstanding taste – "powerful and aromatic, a nose with layers of raisins, brown sugar and blackberries followed by a long creamy finish."

Cocoa pods: Trinidad and Tobago cocoa is unrivalled for its pleasant floral scent and unique taste. *Photo: Oswin Browne*

The old water wheel at Arnos Vale provides a glimpse into Tobago's not too distant past. Photo: Oswin Browne

A rich and turbulent history

It's easy to get a sense of history in Tobago, where old sugar mills, forts and plantation great houses dot the landscape. But if you're looking for the facts behind what some still refer to as Robinson Crusoe's island, start at the Tobago Museum, housed in the old Barrack Guard House in Fort King George, Scarborough.

Tobago may nowadays exude serenity, but there was a period when the comings and goings of European invaders made the 'tranquil isle' one of the busiest in the eastern Caribbean and when the phrase "rich as a Tobago planter" gained currency.

The island that Columbus sighted and named Assumpcion in 1498 was first settled by Arawak-speaking Amerindians from South America around 300BC. By the time the first Europeans arrived in the late 16th century, these Tainos had been replaced by the Kalina, or Island Caribs, who knew the island as 'Tavaco'. Amerindian sites survive at King Peter's, Rockly, Halifax, King's, Queen's, Canoe, Great Courland and Man O'War bays as well as on Little Tobago and even in the grounds of the Arnos Vale nature park.

The Tobago Caribs had no intention of handing over their paradise without a fight. They wiped out the first English settlers (1625) and a party of Dutch in 1628. Although nominally Spanish, the English claimed ownership by virtue of a flag nailed to a tree by some sailors en route to Brazil in 1580, and in 1641 England's Charles I gave Tobago as a christening gift to his godson James, Duke of Courland (today's Latvia).

The Courlanders who arrived the next year met fierce Carib resistance. In 1658 the Dutch (who established Lampsinburg on the site of Scarborough in 1654) captured the Courlanders' Plymouth settlement, renaming it Nieuw Vlissingen.

Maybe sensing the onset of a feeding frenzy, the Caribs retired north as the full European onslaught began. By the time Tobago was finally ceded to Britain in 1814, it had changed hands 31 times. The many forts (Milford, Bennett, James, Granby, French, King George) cannons and tombstones are testimonies to these turbulent times, when if the English, Dutch or French weren't in charge, pirates were.

Following the Dutch seizure of Plymouth in 1658, France's Louis XIV, oblivious to the English claim, granted the Dutch control, who were then driven out by the English who in turn were expelled by the French, who promptly burnt the settlement. Unhappy with French dominance, Britain sent a powerful fleet in 1672, reclaiming the island and establishing a plantation culture driven by African slave labour, producing sugar, cotton and indigo.

The Dutch returned a few years later, largely dismantling the pioneering British efforts in an attempt to appease other competing colonies. Declared a no-man's land by the 1684 Treaty of Aix La Chapelle, Dutch, French and English settlers co-existed peacefully until once again the island became British in 1762 when the House of Assembly was established and work begun on Fort King George. The first capital was founded in 1762 at Mount St George but was abandoned in 1769 for Scarborough.

Subsequently Tobago embarked on a period of rapid development. By 1777 some 80 estates were exporting 160,000 gallons of rum, 24,000 cwt of sugar, 1.5m lbs of cotton and 5,000 lbs of indigo. Out of the 1791 population of 15,020, some 14,170 were slaves who vastly outnumbered the whites and slave revolts were an almost annual affair.

The repercussions of both the French Revolution and the American War of ▶

Fort King George was one of the last colonial forts to be built in Tobago. *Photo: Ian Brierley*

Fort James is located at Plymouth and overlooks Great Courland Bay. It was originally established in the 1650s and is one of Tobago's oldest forts. *Photo: Ian Brierley*

Independence resonated in tiny far-flung Tobago. In 1778 the Americans briefly joined the list of predators and the French returned in 1781. Scarborough was renamed Port Louis and Fort King George became Fort Castries, but as the royalists gave way to the revolutionary republicans, in 1790 the French garrison mutinied, imprisoned their officers and razed Scarborough to the ground.

By 1803 Tobago was finally back in British hands. Initially it prospered but after Emancipation removed its slave labour force in 1838, it sank into economic decline. The removal of protective tariffs on sugar was compounded by the devastating 1847 hurricane and the collapse of the West India Bank which underwrote the plantations. Sharecropping was introduced with reasonable success until the 1870s when planters began reneging on agreements and labour unrest ignited the 1876 Belmanna Riots which began on the Roxborough Estate.

In 1884, Tobago's internal problems took another turn for the worse when the planters received word from London that their commission merchants, A.M. Gillespie & Co, were no longer solvent. Tobago was therefore bankrupt. Subsequently, the once wealthy island was in October 1888 by Order in Council declared an Island Ward of the neighbouring colony of Trinidad, effective 1st January 1889. This was a Colonial Office compromise that as the years went by became increasingly resented in Tobago.

Whatever investment that was made in Tobago by the larger 'sister' was dictated more by necessity than anything else. Tobago's economy stuttered on through agriculture and little else, although in the years after World War Two the island's tourism potential began to be realised. Thirteen months after Independence was declared in August 1962 Hurricane Flora struck and the island's agricultural economic base was once again devastated. Recovery was slow and it did not help that Prime Minister Williams preferred to take Tobagonians off the land and have them employed in the 'Special Works' programme, a system that had been established primarily in Trinidad to mitigate unemployment.

However, by the late 1960s foreign investors had begun to build hotels and create more sustainable employment for Tobagonians. In 1970, both islands were convulsed by the Black Power movement. Tobago's prominent MP, ANR Robinson, who had been Trinidad and Tobago's first Minister of Finance and later the Minister of Foreign Affairs, broke irrevocably with Williams over the latter's handling of the crisis. Returning to Tobago, Robinson formed his own party and in 1976 the Democratic Action Congress won both the Tobago parliamentary seats in the election.

The subsequent displeasure and indifference shown by Williams towards Tobago enabled Robinson to agitate for the re-establishment of the Tobago House of Assembly (THA) and this was achieved in 1980, with Robinson becoming its first Chairman. (Robinson later became Prime Minister of Trinidad and Tobago and ultimately President.)

The THA has increasingly allowed the people of Tobago to have a voice in matters that are relevant to them. At present, there is an intense effort being made to have Tobago granted full internal self-government and to have the status of the Assembly constitutionally reflected. Looking to the future, attempts are being made to diversify the economy and agriculture may well see a comeback. Meanwhile, the economic potential of exploiting the natural gas reserves that lie off Tobago to the benefit of the island's residents in the future cannot be overestimated. As to Tobago's political future, should the island be given the internal powers that are being sought, the strained relationship that has existed between the two islands since 1889 will likely become more comfortable, moving forward as the late President Sir Ellis Clarke once put it: "Side by side, not one behind the other."

Simon Lee

St Patrick Anglican Church was consecrated in 1843 and is the oldest Anglican church in Tobago
Photo: Oswin Browne

Religious rites and practices

Pre-emancipation, West African rites, beliefs and practices dominated among the island's population of enslaved peoples. Today this domination is reflected in the many aspects of African survivals and retentions that are identifiable in current religious practices, folk lore, myths, language, food, art, music, song and dance. Despite this dominance, the religious landscape of Tobago is very diverse with an array of traditional orthodox churches, sects, Ministries, Evangelists and Pentecostalists.

One of the dominant faiths is the Spiritual (Shouter) Baptists. The emergence of the Shouter Baptist Faith that developed alongside the "Shango" religion, what is now known as Orisha, is the clearest evidence of African retentions in Tobago's culture. This was a dynamic collision of African and Caribbean culture that challenged the dominance and orthodoxy of the European religions.

The Anglican, Catholic and Moravian churches weathered the storm but were eventually forced to introduce traditional ways of worship to attract their congregation. The Festival of Harvest for example is celebrated throughout the island. An important aspect of the event is the African concept of putting aside a space, having it cleaned and decorated before the sharing of food and drink. There is also singing and rejoicing.

The Seventh Day Adventists, Pentecostals, Open Bible, Church of God and other independent churches continue to develop throughout the island but steer an independent line to the practices and belief systems of the traditional churches.

Travellers to Tobago would find a visit to a Spiritual Baptist Shouter church very enlightening. Spiritual Baptists have got the gift of imagination; they frequently have dreams and visions and "travel" into the Spirit World. In the process of encountering God's world, they use their minds and bodies in rhythmic song, music and dance to be transported in this journey.

I have experienced such a journey when Mother Clarissa of Black Rock, a matriarch of the Faith, used music as a spiritual tool to draw power from the spiritual world and in the process "travel" to West Africa. There was a complete change in the church setting. Members took on different roles. They all spoke in the same language, hailing out aloud and greeting each other. The drumming was able to lift some members up and set them down again.

Mother Clarissa kept spinning with a tray of food on her head which never fell. Some climbed, others move vertically and horizontally, slowly and rapidly until they were transported back to the original scene. After speaking in a West African tongue to which others responded, Mother Clarissa died off in the spirit and later returned to normal.

Today, worshippers in Tobago can find almost any place of worship to practice their faith including the island's only Mosque in Lowlands or its oldest Anglican Church, St Patrick, consecrated in 1843, at Mt. Pleasant.

The Reverend Patricia Stephens, author of The Spiritual Baptist Faith: African New World Religion

UNITY OF BRETHREN

At the close of the 18th Century a unique group of missionaries from eastern Europe – followers of the reformist John Hus, who was martyred in 1415 – founded the Moravian Church in Tobago. After enormous trials and tribulations the church began to contribute to the general improvement of the lives of Tobago's enslaved communities by building schools (the first at Mt Gomery) and teaching skills like music, sewing and building trades in many of the villages, some of which retain the names that originated from the Moravian faith – Moriah, Salem and Bethesda to name a few.

Beautifully restored examples of their original churches can be found at Black Rock (above) and also at Spring Gardens (right) on Orange Hill Road.

Photos: Oswin Browne
Words: Leslie Palmer, Publisher, 'What's on in Tobago' & London's Notting Hill Carnival pioneer

Ethiopian Orthodox Church in Black Rock
Photo: Stephen Broadbridge

Sacred Heart Roman Catholic Church at Delaford
Photo: Ian Brierley

The Telephone Exchange building is
a dominant edifice in Scarborough
Photo: Stephen Broadbridge

Scarborough: Tobago's vibrant capital

A charmingly unpretentious mix of new and old, Scarborough's friendly and welcoming ambience belies its bloody past. First settled by Dutch merchants as Lampsinsburg in 1654, Tobago's capital has changed names and ownership a dizzying number of times as it ping-ponged back and forth between the Dutch, French and British for 150 years.

In a sense, Scarborough is still characterised by frenetic activity. The deepwater harbour established in 1991 has allowed greater access to shipping, including cruise ships and the fast ferries which provide excellent service to-and-from Port of Spain, and visitor numbers have increased as a result.

Passengers spill onto jostling streets filled with noise and colour and where vendors selling everything from leather goods to fresh fruit and vegetables sit cheek-by-jowl with international food chains. Tin-roofed homes and modern shops cling to the surrounding hillsides in clustered streets which tumble down towards the waterfront.

Leaving the hustle, bustle and heat, a snaking road leads up to the beautifully-preserved Fort King George which sits regally overlooking the town and Rockly Bay 450ft below. The fort's ramparts afford cool breezes and stunning views of the coastline and Atlantic Ocean. Here you will also find the superb Tobago Museum which charts the island's colourful history from Amerindian times.

Scarborough has been Tobago's capital since 1769 and is home to around a third of the island's 54,000 residents, as well as its semi-autonomous seat of governance, the Tobago House of Assembly (reinstituted in 1980 after abolition in 1876).

Shoppers will find all they're looking for, and a few things they weren't, in the capital's shops, markets, street side stalls and Scarborough Mall, but if you're looking for the conveniences of larger-scale mall shopping head to nearby Gulf City Lowlands Mall, which includes a MovieTowne multiplex cinema.

Those staging theatrical and cultural events are eagerly anticipating the completion of the 5,000-capacity Shaw Park Cultural Complex, whilst major sporting events are held at the Dwight Yorke Stadium, a short drive from town.

A warm welcome awaits any visiting cruiser to this twin-island state. For those of you who have not been here before, there are significant differences between Tobago and Trinidad and once you have spent some time here you will surely know about them!

Tobago is relatively laid back and tranquil with lovely clear seas, beautiful sandy beaches and gorgeous bays tucked away amongst the lush greenery of the mountains that rise quickly up from the sea. The frigate birds circle high in the skies and the pelicans dive deep into the seas. The snorkelling and diving are wonderful, especially in the north eastern areas. The people are conservative but friendly and welcoming. Today or tomorrow? It's not that important, it's bound to get done eventually. The services available specifically for cruisers are limited but that is part of the charm. Tobago remains un-spoilt.

James Fuller is an award-winning freelance journalist and author

The Port of Scarborough
Photo: Oswin Browne

Scarborough Methodist Church
Photo: Stephen Broadbridge

The 'T&T Spirit' and 'T&T Express' provide daily ferry services between Scarborough and Port of Spain. *Photo: Ian Brierley*

Tobago is one of the four divisions of the Trinidad and Tobago Fire Service. *Photo: Ian Brierley*

Shops on Carrington Street in Scarborough. *Photo: Ian Brierley*

The War Memorial is a place for quiet reflection. The Tobago House of Assembly building in the background is the island's seat of government. *Photo: Ian Brierley*

Trader in Scarborough
Photo: Ian Brierley

Fort King George is the best preserved colonial fort in Tobago. Built by the French in the 1770s, and named Fort Castries until its capture by the British in the 1780s, its elevated position offers spectacular views of Scarborough and the surrounding countryside. *Photo: Oswin Browne*

Custom st

Taking time out from the hustle and bustle of the capital. *Photo: Ian Brierley*

Like many of the world's capitals, Scarborough is a hive of activity. *Photo: Oswin Browne*

TOBAGO HEALTH SERVICES: SUCCESS IN TRANSITION

For a small island with only 54,000 people, Tobago provides a sophisticated level of health services for its population with many striking successes despite some persistent challenges. Tobago inherited a British colonial approach to healthcare delivery with a two-tiered system in which the public system remained the primary delivery arrangement.

In 2009, the Tobago Community Health Department had over 88,000 patient contacts. Immunisation coverage has been one of the major successes of these contacts and rivals that of many first world countries. By 2010 it had achieved 100% coverage for Diphtheria, Poliomyelitis, Tetanus and Hepatitis B immunisations for infants less than 1 year old; the same level was also achieved with measles, mumps, rubella and yellow fever among children reaching 1 year of age.

The Tobago Regional Health Authority (RHA) Oncology Unit was launched in January 2010 and has already had an average of 51 patient encounters per month and a significant reduction in morbidity since its inception. Unlike Trinidad, the Tobago RHA Dental Health Department is quite active with a successful island-wide dental health program centred mainly on children. Nutrition services for adults and children through the Community and Clinical Nutrition Department is also one of the burgeoning successes of the Division of Health and Social Services in Tobago.

The healthcare system has undergone reorganisation in the post colonial era. Tobago inherited a significant degree of autonomy under the Tobago House of Assembly (THA) Act of 1994 and Regional Health Authority (RHA) Act of 1997. The Chairman and Board of the RHA have been granted responsibility for the delivery of medical services through its 19 health centres across the island stretching from Canaan in the South West to Speyside in the North East and its new flagship institution, the Scarborough Hospital. The Secretary of Health and Social Services also has responsibility for Management of Community Health Services whose primary focus is on public health functions. These services include: Food services (inspection, licensing and registration of commercial food establishments), Vector control (rodent and mosquito control especially for malaria control), Environmental services (food, water, air pollution management, collection and disposal of liquid and solid wastes), and approval of building plans in conjunction with the Division of Town and Country Planning. The central government through the Ministry of Health does set national health standards and policies for all RHAs including the Tobago RHA.

Here, modern health care services are delivered to the population including: family planning and pregnancy care, health and wellness screening, mental health care, paediatric care, diabetic services and other chronic disease clinical services.

In the 2012 budget, the central government, the main provider of Tobago government financing, allocated $2.2 billion for THA general revenues. This represents 4% of the National budget.

With optimum allocation of such resources the health status of Tobagonians could be further improved. Even recently the health status of Tobagonians, as reflected in the 2007 estimated infant mortality rate of 8.7 per 1000 live births and crude mortality rate of 6.6 per 1000 population, can be considered quite a success story. In fact, this compares favourably with the estimated infant mortality of 27.7 per 1000 live births in 2011 and crude mortality rate of 8 per 1000 for Trinidad and Tobago.

Prostate health in Tobago deserves special attention. With a disease prevalence of 15% in males' aged 50 – 79 years, it stands as one of the highest prevalence rates for the disease in the world and compares adversely to lower prevalence rates for US men (3.8%) and US Black men (5%) in the same age group. This problem is receiving the urgent attention it deserves.

So overall this small island has experienced a mixture of health services successes and challenges. Effectively dealing with these in the future will stand as a testament to the remarkable resolve of Tobagonians to make their country the premiere success story of the Caribbean in transition and an ideal destination for visitors and investors. *Photo: Ian Brierley*

Words: Michael Belcon, MD, MPH

Known as 'A Festival of Wind', the Tobago Carnival Regatta is an annual sporting fixture which includes wind-surfing, yachting and kite-boarding. The event attracts participants from throughout the Caribbean, North America and Europe. *Photo: Oswin Browne*

Welcome to sporting Paradise!

The banner danced in the balmy, tropical breeze while the ever-present sun and clumps of cumulus clouds perched on their crescendo, seemingly absorbed in the action taking place below. On the grounds of the Bon Accord Recreational Facilities, entranced spectators lounged on the manicured grass gawking at players engaged in plying their trade on a patch provided by Providence. This was the scene at the inaugural Tobago International Masters Football Tournament, one of many Sport Tourism events now stapled to the Tobago events calendar.

The familiar sight of sport tourists, both active and passive, thoroughly lapping up every moment of their bit of Paradise is a clear signal that the word is out. Idyllic Tobago provides a perfect backdrop for most conventional and unconventional sporting events. But you don't have to take our word for it, just tune into one of the leading global sports networks, ESPN, for their coverage of the Tobago International Cycling Classic and the 1.2 Tour of Tobago, which is now a Union Cycliste Internationale (UCI) sanctioned event. Achieving this status paved the way for teams from several other countries to compete in future events.

Tobago is no stranger to international media coverage though, as for the second time the FIFA caravan rolled in, this time bringing the U-17 Women's World Cup to the newly refurbished Dwight Yorke Stadium – the stadium itself being a legacy of the FIFA U-17 Men's World Cup in 2001. Through these small to mid-sized sport tourism events, Tobagonians have benefitted from world class facilities, equipment, training and exposure to international competition. The tennis hard courts at Shaw Park are a shining example of this benignant legacy.

What is remarkable, however, is not the physical legacy left by these sporting events, but rather the spirit with which competition takes place with this 300 km^2 Caribbean gem as its backdrop. This spirit is embodied in the attitude of the sport tourists. Footballers on the losing end of a match at the Bago Sports Beach Football Invitational walk away with smiles on their faces; fishermen ending the day without a catch at the Tobago Game Fishing Tournament or the Trinidad and Tobago Game Fishing Association (TTGFA) International Game Fishing Tournament disembark from their vessels laughing; triathletes and paddlers struggling to compete with the best at the Rainbow Warriors Triathlon and the Inaugural Dragon Boat Regatta vow to return for the next year.

Based on this spirit, it becomes abundantly evident that across the board, sporting events in Tobago are not merely about the competition as much as they are about the experience of competing in the Capital of Paradise. Indeed…Welcome to Sporting Paradise!

Kwesi DesVignes works in the Events Department of the Tourism Division of the Tobago House of Assembly

Tobago Plantations Golf and Country Club – Like no other course in the world, this course of just over 7000 yards has been designed to reflect its glorious Caribbean landscape. The flat terrain has been sensitively modified to utilise indigenous plants and increase the habitat diversity for wildlife and has been planned around mature trees and landscape features. *Photo: Oswin Browne*

The annual Tobago Carnival Regatta attracts yacht racers from throughout the Caribbean and the rest of the world. *Photo: Oswin Browne*

The Dwight Yorke Stadium was constructed for the 2001 FIFA U-17 World Football Championship which was hosted by Trinidad and Tobago. The 7,500-capacity stadium also hosted the 2005 Carifta Track and Field Championships and hosted the FIFA U-17 Women's Football World Cup in 2010. *Photo: Oswin Browne*

The Tobago Cycling Classic was established in 1986 by a group of Tobagonians to provide an alternative to the traditional sporting interests of cricket, football and athletics. From its original one-day event, it has grown into a five-stage international competition that attracts participants from no fewer than thirty countries. *Photo: Oswin Browne*

The impressive facility at Shaw Park in Scarborough offers eight tennis courts, a basketball court, netball court and ample spectator seating. *Photo: Oswin Browne*

The Great Race at Store Bay
Photo: Oswin Browne

Tobago's Pigeon Point is fast becoming a mecca for kite-boarders through its annual Carnival Regatta. This exhilarating sport, which is the fastest wind-assisted sport, attracts boarders from throughout the globe. *Photo: Oswin Browne*

Tobago's dive sites are unrivalled anywhere in the Caribbean. *Photo: Oswin Browne*

DIVING IN TOBAGO

Photos by Ryan P. Mannette

Whether for competitive sport or recreation, in the island's warm and inviting waters, Scuba Diving is a popular pastime. The nutrient rich waters provide a safe haven for its abundant and diverse marine life, creating unique dive sites unrivalled anywhere in the Caribbean. Whether you are a first time diver or an advanced sports person, there are dive sites around the island suited to you. The Association of Tobago Dive Operators (ATDO) lists numerous scuba diving facilities, some of which are listed here, but visit their website for more details: www.tobagoscubadiving.com.

Dive sites recommended by ATDO

Cove Reef

Cove Reef is a fringing reef that mainly consists of sponges and hard corals. The reef flat starts in 10 metres and is sloping gently down to 25 m. It is one of the deeper reefs in the South end of the island. With its numerous crevices and caves it is the perfect hideaway for lobsters, moray eels and nurse sharks. The typical Caribbean variety can also be found here: Grouper, Trumpet Fish, Rays, Trunk and Trigger Fish, Turtles and Barracudas are dwellers on Cove Reef.

Flying gurnard

Flying Reef

Flying Reef is one of the most popular reefs in Tobago. Due to its length and depth of only 16 metres it is suitable for beginners and advanced divers. A forest of soft corals and enormous sponges dominate the underwater scenery - and if you are looking for more have a look at the vast variety of different reef fish such as Triggerfish, Stingrays, Moray eels, Rainbow Parrotfish, Angelfish, Butterfly Fish, Porcupine Fish, Turtles and much more.

Divers Dream

Divers Dream is a plateau, roughly 5 km offshore. The top of the reef is as shallow as 6m and slopes down to a depth of 25m. Beautifully covered boulders are found in this area, attracting a huge amount of barracudas, snappers, giant parrotfish and triggerfish. Being such an exposed dive site you also can find nurse sharks, eagle rays and reef sharks.

Golden tail moray eel

M.S. Maverick

The ferry "Scarlett Ibis" was sunk in 1997 creating an artificial reef to boost the islands dive product. The 70 meter long ship which was renamed the "Maverick" is sitting upright on a sandy bottom at a maximum depth of 30 meters. In her years under water she has put on a beautiful coat of corals and sponges which is accompanied by schools of bait fish who find shelter in the huge belly of the ship. Jacks are also attracted by this never ending stock of prey available.

The Sisters

The Sisters are 5 pinnacles coming up from more than 40 meters depth. Beautiful covered and bizarre underwater scenery makes the Sisters a memorable dive. In overhangs and caves you find not only lobster but also stingrays and nurse sharks. Depending on the season and current a school of hammerhead sharks can be seen here. The Sisters are fully exposed to the wind and open sea so that it can only be dived in favourable weather conditions.

Japanese Garden

This dive will expose you to the vast variety of marine life in Tobago's waters. After descending into the "fish soup" you will drift towards "Kamikaze Cut" and once passed, you are diving through four different zones of underwater scenery. A dive second to none!

Green turtle

Kelleston Drain

This dive is famous for the huge brain coral at the end of this challenging dive. The nutrient rich water allows a luxuriant growth of sponges and soft coral. Big schools of Creole wrasse and jack fish are always there. Nurse sharks and giant green moray eels are frequently seen on this dive.

Hyperbaric Facility

There is a Hyperbaric facility at the Roxborough Medical Clinic that is used to treat decompression sickness from diving. It's approximately 20 minutes drive from Speyside (northeast) and 40 minutes drive from Scarborough (southwest).

Flamingo tongue feeding on a sea fan

TOBAGO'S SPORTING CALENDAR

A feast of events for everyone whether spectator or participant - the professional, the enthusiast or the amateur.

The Carib Beer Great Race
Organised by the T&T Power Boat Association, this is a 93 mile long race from Carenage in Trinidad to Tobago each August ending at the Scarborough Esplanade.

Tobago Carnival Regatta
A constantly expanding and improving event organised by Tobago Regattas Limited, known as The Festival of the Wind at Pigeon Point in February.

Flying Colours Kite Festival
This is a colourful fiesta of kite flying for pleasure and in competition where you can see all makes of kites including the ubiquitous 'mad bull' kite at Speyside and Plymouth.

Game Fishing
The variety of fish in the seas around Tobago, whether fishing offshore or inshore, is sufficient to meet the needs of any fishing enthusiast.

There are two major tournaments – The Tobago International Game Fishing Tournament held at Charlotteville in March and the Trinidad and Tobago Game Fishing Association Tournament with its International 'Marlin Madness' Tournament in April.

Cricket
Cricket in all its versions are played all over the island but for first class games Scarborough's Shaw Park is the place to be.

Football
Like cricket, you will see football being played wherever there is an open space but at The Dwight Yorke Stadium in Bacolet you will see competitive games.

Rainbow Cup International Triathlon
Celebrating its 8th year in May 2012, this event includes an Olympic & Sprint Triathlon, a Kids Duathlon, a 2,000m Open Water Swim and a 5km Fun Run at Turtle Beach, Black Rock.

Tobago Power Boat Regatta
At Scarborough Esplanade in March.

Yachting
The official ports of entry to Tobago are Scarborough or Charlotteville. Popular anchorage sites can be found at Store Bay, Grafton Beach, Englishman's Bay, Mt Irvine Bay and Anse Bateau.

Golf
Golf is very popular in Tobago. There are two 18-hole golf courses at Mt Irvine Hotel and Tobago Plantations. There are a number of special tournaments that attract both celebrities and professionals – The Dwight Yorke Invitational Golf Tournament (June), The Presidents Cup Golf Tournament (September) and The Chief Secretary's Golf Tournament (September).

Tobago International Cycling Classic
Celebrated its 25th anniversary in 2011, this gruelling road race in October lasts for over four hours. It also includes the Union Cycliste Internationale (UCI), the world's governing body for cycling, 1.2 Tour of Tobago; a total of 112km over 6 mountain tops.

Pirogue Festival

A fun day of boat races for the whole family at Man O'War Bay in Charlotteville in November.

Surfing

The season is from November to April and the favourite places for the experienced surfer are Bacolet and Mt Irvine.

Goat & Crab Racing

A unique sporting event at Buccoo and Mt. Pleasant villages, each Easter, where goats and crabs race along a grass-covered track.

Horseback Riding

Tobago has a couple of stables offering a variety of activities from therapeutic rides to trekking through the countryside or along beaches. The two main stables are:

Being With Horses in Tobago which is located in Buccoo.
Visit www.being-with-horses.com for more information.

Friendship Stables is located in Canaan, Tobago.
Visit www.friendshipridingstables.com for more information.

Mountain Biking

Tobago offers a wide range of trails from breathtaking downhills, challenging single tracks to easy-coast cruises. It is a first class destination for mountain bikers of all levels. There are many natural trails overlooking the ocean with breathtaking views, some of which lead to secluded beaches where riders can cool down and even take a swim before heading to the next trail.

Off Road Tours

There's no better way to see the lay of the land than jumping on a Motorcycle or hopping on the back of the Off-Road Jeeps for a Safari on the winding roadside tour of the island.

The Jeep Safaris allow you to cover parts of the island and appreciate sights that most visitors never get to discover. You will be driven on dirt roads off the beaten track, through rivers and old plantations from the Caribbean coast into the heart of the island.
Visit www.tobagonow.com/tour01.htm or www.alibaba-tours.com/rainforest.htm for more information.

The on and off-road motorcycle tours cater for all needs - learners, intermediate and advanced riders. You can have a custom, individually guided tour taking you to specific areas of interest or in groups of three or more riders. Of course, you can even tour as a passenger rather than a rider.
Visit www.traildogztobago.com for more information.

In addition to any of the above sporting events, visitors can participate in a variety of popular sports at venues all over the island. These include various watersports, lawn tennis, athletics, basketball, hockey, rugby, table tennis, volleyball, netball and horse riding.

For up to date information on the major events in Tobago, get the free booklet, 'What's on ... in Tobago' or see www.whatsonintobago.com.

Photo: Dragon Boat Regatta by Oswin Browne

Tobago is one of the world's leading dive destinations
Photo courtesy Tourism Development Company (TDC)

The perfect choice for your next visit

The inauguration of the Tobago House of Assembly in 1980 resulted in tourism becoming the focus because of an environment offering peace, quiet, relaxation and safety. This was boosted by the island's natural beauty consisting of but not limited to, the flora and fauna, beaches, the coral reef, a world renowned rainforest, the culture and the hospitality of the people.

The ANR Robinson International Airport is located 7 miles (10km) from Scarborough and is serviced by the following airlines:

- British Airways. Direct flights from Gatwick, London. Reservations: 1 800 452 1201 / 800 744 2477. www.ba.com

- Caribbean Airlines. Weekly service from New York and hourly services to Trinidad. Reservations: 1 868 625 7200. www.caribbean-airlines.com

- Virgin Atlantic. Direct flights from Gatwick, London. Reservations: 1 800 744 7477. www.virgin-atlantic.com

- Monarch. Direct flights from Gatwick, London. Reservations: 1 868 639 2285/ 1103. www.monarch.co.uk

- Condor. Weekly service from Frankfurt, Germany. Reservations: 1 868 639 2285 / 1103, reservation.en@condor.com. www.condor.com

There are two fast ferries (T&T Express and T&T Spirit) and one conventional ferry (Warrior Spirit) travelling daily between Trinidad and Tobago.

But you cannot go wrong by choosing Tobago for your next visit because this little island is not just clean, green and serene but boasts of the following:

- A range of offers of leisure, event, conference, festival and heritage tourism.
- A religious and cultural diversity unrivalled in the Caribbean with unique aspects of African cultural retentions that resulted in a rich inheritance of dance, music, art, cuisine and festivals.
- An International variety of culinary delights, alongside a mixture of indigenous and fusion cuisine as no other destination can boast.
- The lead Caribbean destination for eco-tourism; Tobago has the oldest protected rainforest in the Western Hemisphere (designated on 17 April 1776); Two out of the three sites designated as Wetlands of International Importance – Tobago's Buccoo Reef and The Bon Accord Lagoon Complex.
- The major nesting sites of the critically endangered leather back sea turtle. These majestic animals come ashore to deposit their eggs between March and September every year.
- Unique opportunities to see rare and exotic species of flora and fauna – Oncidium citrinum orchids, Leatherback Turtles and Bats.
- Tobago has pristine beaches and the best dive sites in the Eastern Caribbean
- Enhanced safety and security services at all beaches and tourism sites.
- Trained and experienced service personnel; e.g. Tourist taxi drivers are trained and certified to national standards of quality with annual auditing and re-certification.

Pigeon Point Beach
Photo: Richard Bhagan

Mount Irvine Bay Golf Course is an award-winning, championship quality, 18-hole course with spectacular views of the Caribbean Sea. Established in 1968, it was carved out from the grounds of an old coconut plantation and is regarded as one of the leading golf courses in the Caribbean. *Photo: Oswin Browne*

'Optimist Sailors' prepare their boats for competition in the Tobago Carnival Regatta. *Photo: Oswin Browne*

Established in 1898, the botanical gardens in Scarborough occupy seventeen acres of well-tendered shrubs, trees and tropical gardens. *Photo: Oswin Browne*

Situated along a two-and-a-half mile stretch of beach and coastline, the Magdalena Grand Beach Resort is part of the Tobago Plantations Estate, a 750-acre community of luxury villas, condominiums and bungalows. *Photo: Oswin Browne*

Beach bar at the popular Pigeon Point
Photo: Ian Brierley

Known as the "friendliest regatta" in the Caribbean, Tobago Sail Week attracts enthusiasts from throughout the globe. *Photo: Oswin Browne*

Mt Irvine Bay is a popular location for surfers
Photo: Oswin Browne

Powerboat racing during the Tobago Carnival Regatta
Photo: Oswin Browne

Kite-boarders at Pigeon Point during the Tobago
Carnival Regatta. *Photo: Oswin Browne*

Walking down the aisle is a major highlight in your wedding. What if that aisle is a golden beach, a historic fort or a sun-draped glade set in the lush rainforest? A Tobago Wedding offers you all of this and more – a backdrop of turquoise seas, exquisite sunsets and enchanting moonlit nights. Your Tobago Wedding will be a memory of a lifetime in Truly Romantic Tobago. *Photo: Oswin Browne*

GETTING MARRIED IN TOBAGO

Couples intending to get married in Tobago will need to purchase a Special Marriage Licence. This is available from the Inland Revenue Department, Sangsters Hill, Scarborough. To be eligible for such a licence, couples must comply with the following:

- Both parties must be non-residents of Trinidad and Tobago with a valid return ticket
- They must reside in Tobago for at least three days prior to the marriage
- If divorced, original or notarised copy of Decree Absolute must be available
- If widowed, the original death certificate of spouse must be available

- Proof of name change must be available where name differs on documents
- Persons under age 18 must have documented consent from a parent or legal guardian
- Documents must be in English or translated into English and notarised
- The wedding ceremony must be conducted by 6pm
- Two witnesses with their own ID (passport) must be present

NB. All marriages are considered civil except Orisha, Hindu and Muslim ceremonies which have additional requirements. Most countries automatically recognise a Tobago marriage as legal. However, visitors are advised to check the requirements of their country with regard to overseas marriages

Tobago is at a crossroad in its development and a serious effort has had to be
made to diversify the island's economic base. *Photo: Stephen Broadbridge*

Stable investment opportunities

A look at Tobago today will demonstrate there have been leaps and bounds in its development process. The island boasts a sound and stable administration, a well developed infrastructure, dependable utilities, a sound ferry service on the sea bridge with Trinidad and an international airport connecting it with the rest of the region and the world.

Today's Tobago, however, is at a crossroad in its development and with the exploding expansion, a serious effort has had to be made to diversify the island's economic base. In recent times, attention has been turned to the establishment of 'Cove Eco-Industrial Estate and Business Park'. This initiative is the brainchild of the Tobago House of Assembly and really offers a virgin business environment to entrepreneurs. The Estate offers opportunities to investors to get involved in light industry. It will accommodate knowledge-based industries including information technology, light manufacturing, agro-processing and export as well as selected downstream activities related to natural gas. It will also house receiving and metering facilities for natural gas from Trinidad.

Investment at this park is encouraged through a series of tax holidays, incentives and exemptions. What is even more significant is the fact that, in 2008, there was a natural gas discovery on the island's North West. This will definitely result in the provision of a secure energy base which will drive the Estate initiative and make investment on the island a promise that will be fulfilled.

In addition, investing in Tobago is a low risk opportunity because of the following features of the island:

- Strategic geographical location: Gateway to South and North America with good access to developing & emerging markets and at the southern tip of the hurricane belt.
- Regulated financial system with competitive fiscal incentives and no foreign exchange controls.
- Good infrastructure and full range of support services for secondary industries which includes information technology, telecoms, construction, training, business & accounting, research & testing.
- A strong democratic tradition with a pro-investment business climate and very stable political system.
- Low energy and competitive raw material costs.
- International confidence in economic resilience and positive economic growth with impressive mid-term strategy to achieve lasting prosperity through innovation, diversification and economic transformation.
- Track record of attracting local, regional and international investment and attention.
- Good living standards with modern and accessible leisure activities and facilities for foreign nationals and their families.
- Educated and highly skilled and trained English-speaking workforce with 99% literacy rate
- Developed Private Sector
- Generous tax holidays, incentives and exemptions, and
- Very stable local economy and growth trends

Pigeon Point beach as viewed from its iconic jetty. The resort has excellent tourism facilities including bars, a restaurant and souvenir shops. *Photo: Ian Brierley*

Tobago Plantations Beach and Golf Resort is a 750-acre community resort that offers a luxury Caribbean lifestyle for the wise investor. The development comprises villas (pictured) and condominiums and a raft of facilities to satisfy every taste, including golf course, driving range, golf and country club, restaurant and bar, conference facilities, spa, health club and beach club to name a few. *Photo: Oswin Browne*

BUYING REAL ESTATE IN TOBAGO

The attractions of Tobago as a touris destination of first choice are the very same reasons why anyone would want to live out thei dream life on this idyllic land that is clean, green and serene.

Property on the lower end of the marke begins at TT $1 million and rise to TT $25 millio for luxury villas. Investment in real estate i encouraged and there are several professiona agencies able to guide you through the variou processes to that dream acquisition.

Ownership of property in Tobago by foreig nationals is regulated by the Foreign Investmen Act 1990 which allows purchasers to buy up t one acre (one parcel only) for a private dwellin house and up to five acres for commercia purposes.

An automatic licence to purchase (subjec to only proof of good character) will be grante on application for all purchases by foreig nationals within certain Designate Development areas. These designated area include: Englishman's Bay Estate, Cullode Estate, parts of Arnos Vale, parts of Grafton Mount Irvine Estate, Buccoo Estate, Golde Grove Estate, Lowlands Estate including Tobag Plantations Resort, Diamond Estate includin Indigo Bay Resort, parts of Bacolet Estate.

Purchases outside these designated area will be discretionary and dealt with on a cas by case basis. Foreign nationals wishing invest in larger properties of over five acres ca apply for a development licence through th Tourism Development Company (TDC). Foreig nationals must purchase in an internationall traded foreign currency and proof of transfer funds is needed by the Ministry of Finance.

Permission to buy land does not confe residency. Buying a commercial property doe not confer the right to work (earn an income) Tobago. Work permits are needed for any wo that lasts longer than 30 days.

If you are intending to live in Tobago, foreig nationals should contact the Trinidad ar Tobago High Commission or embassy in the country for information on immigration and/ work permit requirements.

If you are planning to come on holiday enjoy your new property, a non-resident usually allowed up to three months in Trinida and Tobago, with or without the need for a vis which depends on the country of orig Discretionary extensions can be applied for.

Tobago is not only clean, green and sere but is also very beautiful and very special. It a small island that is ideal for sensitive a sustainable development that does not threat its eco-systems. Any investment you make v be sound and will, with family and friends, op up a whole new vista to relax, enjoy and rene your energies.

The award-winning Coco Reef resort is located on the south-western coast and is no more than five minutes' drive from ANR International Airport. Among its many facilities, the resort benefits from being within walking distance of two of Tobago's most popular beaches – Pigeon Point and Store Bay. *Photo: Oswin Browne*

Scarborough became the capital of Tobago in 1769 and has a population of around 17,000. Its deep-water harbour was built in 1991 and accommodates cruise ships as well as the inter-island ferry service. *Photo: Oswin Browne*

A.N.R. Robinson International Airport is one of two international airports serving the Republic of Trinidad and Tobago; the other being Piarco international Airport in Trinidad. Formerly named Crown Point International Airport, and renamed in 2011, it was opened in 1940 and is located at the southern tip of Tobago. *Photo: Oswin Browne*

Tobago – muy hermoso, muy especial

La isla de Tobago es limpia, verde y tranquila. Una isla pequeña que conserva su encanto natural. Tobago es un destino de primera elección para visitantes y más y más para inversionistas bien informados.

Tobago se encuentra situada a 11 grados de latitud norte, 60 grados de longitud Oeste, a 42 kilómetros al noroeste de su isla gemela Trinidad. Con sólo 42 Km de longitud y 10 Km de latitud con una masa de tierra de 300 Km2 está rodeada por arrecifes de coral. La meseta del suroeste de baja coralina va subiendo gradualmente hacia la cordillera central de colinas volcánicas que alcanzan los 567 metros de altura. Bosques densos (el bosque protegido más antiguo en el hemisferio occidental) se levanta sobre las playas de arena blanca de la costa del Caribe Sotavento y las rocas de la costa del Atlántico Barlovento.

Hasta tiempos geológicos recientes Tobago fue parte del continente de Sur América. Su abundante flora y fauna de la isla y continente incluye: 220 especies de pájaros, 23 tipos de mariposas, 24 serpientes no venenosas, 17 murciélagos, 16 lagartijas, 14 ranas, 12 mámales y 5 tortugas marinas.

Originalmente habitada por indígenas americanos, Tobago subsecuentemente tuvo diversas oleadas colonizadoras Europeas en competencia. Los courlanders llegaron primero en 1642, seguidos por los holandeses, franceses e ingleses, hasta que la isla fue cedida a Britania por el Tratado de Paris de 1802. Tobago llegó a ser una Colonia Británica en 1877, uniéndose a Trinidad como una unidad política en 1888.

La mayoría de la población de 55,000 habitantes son descendientes de los africanos esclavizados importados para trabajar en las plantaciones de azúcar desde finales del Siglo XVII. Las raíces culturales Afro-Criollas sobreviven en el folklore, la música y la cocina, demostrándose en los muchos Festivales a través del año.

La historia colonial rica de la isla, sus recursos naturales bellísimos y su cultura sin igual la hace tan diferente de otros destinos turísticos. Tobago se complementa con servicios bien mantenidos, gente genuinamente amigable y un aeropuerto accesible y está abierto para negocios a todo el mundo.

Los visitantes gozan de dos selvas tropicales – la "selva tropical del mar" y la "selva tropical terrestre"

La isla es el mejor lugar para bucear en el Sureste del Caribe. Los arrecifes de coral ligeramente inclinados, los acantilados submarinos profundos y las formaciones volcánicas ofrecen excitantes zambullidos. Aguas ricas en nutrientes pululan con casi 300 especies de coral duro; una amplia variedad de esponjas; una miríada de peces tropicales; Ballenas, tiburones, delfines, raras manta rayas, calamares y tortugas.

La pequeña aldea de Pescadores de Speyside es en el centro del buceo, con una diversidad de sitios y los vórtices de arroyos de la marea alrededor de las costas de las islas, ideal para zambullirse. La industria del buceo opera con los estándares de seguridad internacional, con servicios de cámara descompresora gratis en Scarborough.

Diferentes lugares provén una complete gama de deportes acuáticos desde el deporte de vela, carreras náuticas, kite surfing y pesca de bromeo; aquellos que prefieren un acercamiento más pausado apreciarán la observación de arrecifes a través de una embarcación con fondo de vidrio, particularmente en Nylon Pool, un área aguamarina poco profunda creada por un banco de arena fuera de la costa en Buccoo Reef.

La "Tierra de la Selva Tropical" es un nirvana verdadero para los naturalistas

Highland Waterfall
Photo: Kyle Walcott

que atraen ornitologistas, naturalistas y eco turistas ávidos de encontrar el emblemático cocrico, caminar a través de la Reserva Forestal, escalar las cascadas o mirar las tortugas por las noches poner sus huevos en la playa. El ciclismo de montaña, en la montaña o fuera de ella es una excelente alternativa al turismo por coche para los aventureros energéticos.

A pesar de toda la tranquilidad, los visitantes todavía pueden encontrar sorpresivamente programas de entretenimiento completo y vida nocturna que frecuentemente muestra la cultura local. La fiesta de la Playa de la Escuela Dominical semanal en Buccoo ha llegado a ser una institución, ya que tiene las únicas carreras de cangrejos y cabras de Pascua. Tobago también presenta varios eventos y festivales internacionales que incluyen Festivales de Comida, Vuelo de Cometas, tamborileo, Modas y Jazz.

La economía, hasta recientemente impulsada por el turismo y la inmobiliaria, se está diversificando a través de proyectos de la industria ligera tales como el Cove-Eco Industrial and Business Park y la resucitación de la antigua industria del cacao en el Tobago Cocoa Estate cerca de Roxborough.

El complejo inmobiliario se promueve activamente con incentivos para la inversión que han contribuido a muchos nuevos desarrollos, incluyendo complejos de grandes hoteles, desarrollo de villa y dos nuevos centros comerciales.

Los visitantes que buscan invertir en Tobago se benefician no solo de estas exenciones sino de las cuotas de inmobiliaria, que les permite tener hasta 2 hectáreas de tierra con fines comerciales sin estatus de residentes.

Tobago es una isla muy bella y muy especial. Bienvenidos a Tobago.

Tobago – muito bonita; muito especial

A ilha de Tobago é limpa, verde e serena. Uma pequena ilha em grande parte preservada, Tobago é a primeira escolha de destino para visitants e, cada vez mais, para aqueles investidores bem informados.

Tobago está localizada a 11 graus de latitude norte, a 60 graus de longitude oeste e a 21 milhas a nordeste de sua ilha-irmã, Trinidad. Com apenas 21 milhas (42 km) de extensão e 7 milhas (10 km) de largura, com um território de 116 milhas quadradas (300 km2), é cercada por recife de corais. O planalto coralino sudoeste de baixa altitude eleva-se gradualmente a uma cordilheira central de colinas vulcânicas atingindo 1.860 pés. A densa floresta tropical (a mais antiga floresta protegida no hemisfério ocidental) se eleva acima das praias de areia branca da costa caribenha de sota-vento e da costa rochosa de barlavento do Atlântico. Até tempos geológicos recentes, Tobago fazia parte do continente sul-americano. Sua terra abundante e a flora e a fauna da ilhas incluem: 220 espécies de aves, 23 de borboletas, 24 de cobras não-venenosas, 17 de morcegos, 16 de lagartos, 14 de sapos, 12 de mamíferos e 5 de tartarugas marinhas.

Originalmente habitada por ameríndios, Tobago foi posteriormente contestada pelas ondas de colonizadores europeus. Curlândios chegaram primeiro em 1642, seguidos pelos holandeses, franceses e ingleses, até que a ilha foi cedida à Grã-Bretanha pelo Tratado de Paris, de 1802. Tobago tornou-se uma colônia da Coroa Britânica em 1877, agregando-se a Trinidad como unidade política em 1888.

A maioria dos 55.000 moradores é descendente de escravos africanos trazidos para trabalhar nas plantações de açúcar a partir do final do século XVII. Raízes culturais afro-crioulas sobrevivem no folclore, na música e na gastronomia apresentados em muitos festivais ao longo do ano.

É a rica história colonial, os impressionantes recursos naturais e a cultura única da ilha que a diferencia de outros destinos turísticos. Juntamente com instalações bem conservadas, pessoas verdadeiramente amigáveis e um aeroporto acessível, Tobago está aberta para negócios para todo o mundo. Os visitantes desfrutarão de duas florestas tropicais – a "floresta tropical do mar" e "floresta tropical da terra".

A ilha é o melhor local de mergulho do sudeste do Caribe. Recifes de coral levemente inclinados, falésias submarinas acentuadas e formações vulcânicas oferecem mergulhos emocionantes. Águas ricas em nutrientes fervem com cerca de 300 espécies de corais duros, uma grande variedade de esponjas, uma miríade de peixes tropicais, baleias, tubarões, golfinhos, raras raias manta, lulas e tartarugas.

A pequena aldeia de pescadores de Speyside é central para mergulho, com uma diversidade de locais e o turbilhão de correntes marítimas ao redor das ilhas ideais para mergulhos à deriva. A indústria de mergulho é operada segundo as normas de segurança internacionais, com instalação de câmara de descompressão de uso gratuito em Scarborough.

Locais diferentes atendem a toda a gama de esportes aquáticos, de vela e competição de lanchas de alta velocidade à prática de kitesurf e pesca esportiva; aqueles que preferem uma proposta mais vagarosa apreciarão encontrar recifes através de barcos com fundo de vidro, principalmente em Nylon Pool, uma área rasa verde-azulada criada por um banco de areia fora da costa em Buccoo Reef.

A "floresta tropical da terra" é um nirvana virtual para os naturalistas, a qual

atrai ornitólogos, naturalistas e ecoturistas ansiosos para ver o emblemático aracuã (ortalis ruficauda), fazer trilhas pela reserva florestal, escalar cachoeiras ou ver a desova de tartarugas na praia, à noite. Para os energeticamente aventureiros, o mountain biking na estrada de terra é uma excelente alternativa ao passeio de carro.

Apesar de toda a tranquilidade, os visitantes ainda encontrarão, surpreendentemente, uma completa programação de entretenimento e vida noturna que, com frequência, mostra a cultura local. A semanal festa da Sunday School, na praia, em Buccoo tornou-se uma tradição, assim como as excepcionais corridas de bode e de caranguejo na Páscoa. Tobago também é palco de vários festivais e eventos internacionais que incluem festivais gastronômicos, de pipas, de percussão, de moda e de jazz.

A economia, até recentemente impulsionada principalmente pelo turismo e corretagem de imóveis, está se diversificando através de leves projetos industriais, como o Parque Industrial e Empresarial Cove-Eco e a reanimação da indústria do cacau no antigo Tobago Cocoa Estate, perto de Roxborough. O desenvolvimento imobiliário é ativamente encorajado com incentivos ao investimento, os quais têm contribuído para as muitas novas urbanizações, incluindo grandes complexos hoteleiros, condomínios de casas de veraneio e dois novos shoppings.

Os visitantes que procuram investir em Tobago se beneficiam não somente de isenções, mas também de uma cota imobiliária, o que lhes permite ter até cinco acres de terra para fins comerciais, sem o estado de residente.

Tobago é uma ilha muito bonita e muito especial. Bem-vindo a Tobago.

Tobago –île très belle ; très spéciale

L'île de Tobago est propre, verte et paisible. Une petite île, largement préservée, Tobago est une destination de premier choix pour les visiteurs et de plus en plus pour les investisseurs avisés.

Tobago se situe à une latitude de 11 degrés nord et une longitude de 60 degrés ouest, à 42 kilomètres au nord-est de son île sœur, la Trinité. Avec seulement 42 kilomètres de long sur 10 kilomètres de large et une surface de 300 kilomètres carrés, l'île est entourée de récifs coralliens. Le plateau de corail bas au sud-ouest s'élève progressivement à une chaîne centrale de collines volcaniques atteignant 567 mètres. Une forêt tropicale dense (la plus ancienne forêt protégée de l'hémisphère occidental) s'élève au-dessus des plages de sable blanc de la côte caribéenne sous le vent et du littoral rocheux de la partie au vent de l'Atlantique.

Jusqu'aux temps géologiques récents, Tobago faisait partie du continent sud-américain. Son abondante flore et faune continentales et insulaires comprennent : 220 espèces d'oiseaux, 23 papillons, 24 serpents non vénéneux, 17 chauves-souris, 16 lézards, 14 grenouilles, 12 mammifères et 5 tortues marines.

Initialement habitée par les Amérindiens, Tobago a été ultérieurement disputée par des vagues de colons européens. Les Courlandais étaient les premiers à arriver en 1642, suivis par les Hollandais, les Français, et les Anglais, avant d'être cédée à la Grande-Bretagne par le Traité de Paris de 1802. Tobago est devenue une colonie de la couronne britannique en 1877, rejoignant la Trinité en tant qu'unité politique en 1888.

La plupart de la population de 55.000 est composée de descendants d'esclaves africains importés pour travailler sur les plantations de canne à sucre à partir de la fin du XVIIe siècle. Les racines culturelles afro-créoles perdurent dans le folklore, la musique et la gastronomie, qui sont présentés dans de nombreux Festivals au cours de l'année.

Ce sont l'histoire coloniale riche, les ressources naturelles remarquables et la culture unique de cette île qui la distinguent des autres destinations touristiques. Grâce à ces dernières, associées à des installations bien entretenues, un peuple vraiment accueillant et un aéroport accessible, Tobago est ouverte aux affaires du monde entier.

Les visiteurs profiteront de deux forêts tropicales – la « forêt tropicale maritime » et la « forêt tropicale terrestre ».

L'île est le principal site de plongée de la Caraïbe du sud-est. Les récifs coralliens en pente douce, falaises sous-marines plongeantes et formations volcaniques offrent des plongées excitantes. Les eaux riches en nutriments grouillent de presque 300 espèces de coraux durs, une grande variété d'éponges, d'innombrables poissons tropicaux, des baleines, requins et dauphins, raies Manta rares, calamars et tortues.

Le petit village de pêche de Speyside est un centre de plongée important, avec une diversité de sites et un tourbillon de courants de marée autour des îles au large de la côte – idéaux pour la plongée dérivante. L'industrie de la plongée est exécutée conformément aux normes internationales de sécurité, avec un service gratuit de chambres de décompression à Scarborough.

Différents lieux offrent la gamme entière de sports aquatiques, y compris la voile, les courses de bateaux à moteur, le kite surf et la pêche ; ceux qui préfèrent une approche plus décontractée pourront profiter des récifs à partir des bateaux à fond de verre, notamment à Nylon Pool, une zone bleue verte peu profonde créée par un banc de sable au large de la côte à Buccoo Reef.

La « forêt tropicale terrestre » est un véritable paradis des naturalistes ; elle attire des ornithologues, naturalistes et écotouristes avides de voir le cocrico emblématique, de faire des randonnées à travers la réserve forestière, escalader les cascades ou observer les tortues nichant sur la plage durant la nuit. Pour les aventuriers énergiques, le vélo de montagne sur et hors route est une excellente alternative au tourisme en voiture.

Malgré toute la sérénité, les visiteurs y trouveront aussi, à leur grande surprise, un programme de divertissement rempli et une vie nocturne qui présente souvent la culture locale. La Sunday School Beach Party, fête de plage hebdomadaire le dimanche à Buccoo, est devenue une institution, tout comme les courses uniques de chèvres et de crabes à Pâques. Tobago accueille aussi de nombreux Festivals et événements internationaux, y compris des Festivals de Nourriture, de Cerfs-volants, de Tambours et de Jazz.

L'économie, impulsée notamment par le tourisme et l'immobilier jusqu'à récemment, est en train de se diversifier grâce à des projets industriels légers comme le parc industriel et commercial Cove-Eco et la renaissance de l'industrie ancienne du cacao au Tobago Cocoa Estate près de Roxborough.

Le développement de l'immobilier est activement encouragé, à l'aide d'incitations à l'investissement, qui ont contribué aux nombreux nouveaux projets, y compris les grands complexes hôteliers, ensembles de villas et deux nouveaux centres commerciaux.

Les visiteurs souhaitant investir à Tobago profiteront non seulement de ces exemptions mais aussi d'un quota immobilier, qui leur permettra de posséder jusqu'à 2 hectares de terrain à des fins commerciales sans avoir le statut de résident.

Tobago est une île très belle et très spéciale. Bienvenue à Tobago.

Tobago – wunderschön, einzigartig

Die Insel Tobago ist sauber, grün und ruhig. Eine kleine weitgehend unverdorbene Insel, Tobago ist ein Reiseziel der ersten Wahl für Besucher und zunehmend für Investoren.

Tobago liegt am Breitengrad von 11 N, Längengrad 60 W und 21 Meilen Nordost ihrer Schwesterinsel Trinidad. Die Insel ist nur 21 Meilen (42 km) lang und 7 Meilen (10 km) breit mit einer Landmasse von 116 Quadratmeilen (300 km²) und von Korallenriffen umgeben. Das südwestliche Plateau mit tiefliegenden Korallenalgen steigt allmählich zum mittleren Bergkamm der vulkanischen Berge und erreicht bis zu 1.860 Fuss. Dichter Regenwald (das älteste Naturschutzgebiet in der westlichen Hemisphäre) erhebt sich über die weißen Sandstränden im Windschatten der karibischen Küste und der felsigen Küstenlinie des windgewandten Atlantiks.

Noch bis vor wenigen Jahren der geologischen Entwicklung war Tobago ein Teil des südamerikanischen Kontinents. Zu der am Festland und auf der Insel befindlichen vielfältigen Pflanzen- bzw. Tierwelt gehören: 220 Vogelarten, 23 verschiedene Schmetterlinge, 24 ungiftige Schlangenarten, 17 Sorten Fledermäuse, 16 Eidechsenarten, 14 verschiedene Froscharten, 12 Säugetierarten und 5 unterschiedliche Arten von Meeresschildkröten.

Ursprünglich von Amerindianern bewohnt, wurde Tobago später mit Strömen von kolonisierenden Europäern besiedelt. Zuerst sind die Courlanders im Jahr 1642 auf der Insel gelandet, gefolgt von den Holländern, Franzosen,Engländern, bis die Insel 1802 durch den Pariser Vertrag an Großbritannien abgetreten wurde. Im Jahr 1877 wurde Tobago eine britische Kronkolonie und in Verbindung mit Trinidad im Jahr 1888 eine politische Einheit.

Die Mehrheit der 55.000 Einwohner sind Nachkommen verschleppter Afrikaner, die Anfang des 17. Jahrhunderts und darüber hinaus zum Arbeiten in den Zuckerrohrplantagen importiert wurden. Afrokreolische kulturelle Wurzeln leben weiter in der Folklore, Musik und Küche, die in vielen Festen das ganze Jahre hindurch präsentiert werden.

Die lange Kolonialgeschichte der Insel sowie ihre Naturschätze und einzigartige Kultur, die sie von allen anderen Reisezielen klar hervorhebt. Zusammen mit gepflegten Einrichtungen, aufrichtigen freundlichen Menschen und einem leicht zugänglichen Flughafen, steht Tobago der ganzen Welt verkaufsoffen.

Besucher werden zwei Regenwälder geniessen können– der „Regenwald des Meeres" und der „Regenwald auf dem Festland".

Die Insel ist das erstklassige Tauchressort der südöstlichen Karibik. Sanft sich neigende Korallenriffe, tief sinkende Unterwasserklippen und vulkanische Formationen bieten ein atemberaubendes Tauchen. Nährstoffreiche Gewässer, in denen nahezu 300 Arten von Steinkorallen; einer Vielfalt von Schwämmen, unzähligen tropischen Fischen; Walen, Haifischen, Delfinen, seltenen Mantarochen, Tintenfischen und Schildkröten wimmeln.

Das Fischerdorf von Speyside ist ein zentraler Tauchort, mit verschiedenen Tauchstellen und einem Strudel von Gezeitenströmen um die vorgelagerten Inseln, ideal für Drift-Tauchgänge. Die Tauchindustrie wird gemäß den internationalen Sicherheitsvorschriften mit einer kostenlosen Unterdruckkammereinrichtung in Scarborough betrieben.

Coco Reef resort
Photo: Ian Brierley

Verschiedene Stellen bieten eine ganze Reihe von Wassersportarten, von Segeln, Wassermotorsport, Drachensurfen bis hin zu Sportangeln; wer ein viel gemütlicheres Herangehen bevorzugt, wird durch die durchsichtigen Böden der Glasbodenboote die verschiedenen Riffe bewundern können, insbesondere den Nylon Pool, ein aquamarinblauer Flachbereich, der durch eine vorgelagerte Sandbank am Buccoo Reef erzeugt wird.

Der „Regenwald am Festland" ist ein virtuelles Nirwana für Naturalisten, das Ornithologen, Naturalisten sowie Ökotouristen, die eifrig darauf sind, den symbolischen Cocrico zu sichten, durch geschützten Waldgebiet zu wandern, Wasserfälle zu erklettern oder Meeresschildkröten nachts bei Brutaktivitäten im Strandgebiet zu beobachten. Die energetischen abenteuerlustigen Mountainbiketouren bieten eine exzellente Alternative zum Touren mit dem Auto.

Für die Gelassenheit, finden die Besucher noch überraschenderweise ein volles Unterhaltungsprogramm und Nachtleben, die oft die einheimische Kultur darstellt. Die wöchentliche Sunday-School-Strandparty in Buccoo ist eine Institution geworden, ebenfalls die einzigartigen Ziegen- und Krebsrennen zum Ostern. Tobago bietet auch mehrere Feste und internationale Veranstaltungen, die u.a. kulinarische Feste, Drachenfliegen, Trommelspielen, Mode und Jazz beinhalten.

Die Wirtschaft, die bis vor kurzem hauptsächlich durch Tourismus und Immobilien getrieben wurde, verändert sich durch leichte industrielle Projekte wie beispielsweise das Cove-Öko-Industriell- und Gewerbegebiet und die Wiederbelebung der ehemaligen Kakaoindustrie in der Tobago Cocoa Estate in der Nähe von Roxborough.

Die Entwicklung im Immobilienbereich wird aktiv gefördert durch Investitionsanreize, die zu vielen neuen Entwicklungen beigetragen haben, einschließlich großen Hotelanlagen, Villen und zwei neuen Einkaufszentren.

Besucher, die gerne in Tobago investieren wollen, haben nicht nur durch diese Ausnahmeregelungen den Vorteil, sondern auch durch die Immobilienquote, die ihnen erlaubt bis hin zu 5 (fünf) Acres an Gewerbefläche zu besitzen, ohne Aufenthaltsberechtigung.

Tobago ist eine sehr schöne und besondere Insel. „Herzlich Willkommen !" auf Tobago.

TOBAGO HOUSE OF ASSEMBLY DIVISIONS

Tourism and Transportation
12 Sangster's Hill,
Scarborough.
Tel: (868) 639-2125 / 4636
Fax: (868) 639-3566
Web: www.visittobago.gov.tt

Finance, Enterprise Development, Consumer Affairs and Cooperatives
Lot #2, Glen Road.
Tel: (868) 635-1203
Fax: (868) 639-4927

Agriculture, Marine Affairs and the Environment
Tam Building, Glen Road.
Tel: (868) 639-2570
Fax: (868) 639-1746

Community Development & Culture
11 Main Street, Scarborough.
Tel: (868) 639-4009
Fax: (868) 635-1044

Education, Youth Affairs & Sport
Singh's Building, Dutch Fort,
Scarborough.
Tel: (868) 639-4137
Fax: (868) 635-0301

Health and Social Services
Social Welfare Office, Tam
Building, Glen Road.
Tel: (868) 635-0073
Fax: (868) 635-0306

Infrastructure and Public Utilities
Old Government Farm Road,
Shaw Park.
Tel: (868) 639-3126
Fax: (868) 639-2422

Settlements and Labour
Department of Settlements,
Bobtail Building, Smithfield,
Milford Road, Scarborough.
Tel: (868) 660-7473
Fax: (868) 639-2028

DIPLOMATIC REPRESENTATION (Trinidad and Tobago)

Embassy of the Federative Republic of Brazil
Tel: (868) 622-5779 / 5771
Email: embassyofbrazil@tstt.net.tt

High Commission for Canada
Tel: (868) 622-6232 / 2581
Email: pspan@international.gc.ca

Embassy of the Republic of Chile
Tel: (868) 628-0540 / 4763
Email: echile@tstt.net.tt

Embassy of the People's Republic of China
Tel: (868) 622-6976
Email: chinaembtt@mfa.gov.cn

Embassy of the Republic of Costa Rica
Tel: (868) 628-0652 / 0653
Email: emticatt@trinidad.net

Embassy of the Republic of Cuba
Tel: (868) 622-6075 / 9142
Email: embacubatrinidad@tstt.net.tt

Embassy of the Dominican Republic
Tel: (868) 624-7930
Email: embadom@hotmail.com

Delegation of the European Union to Trinidad and Tobago
Tel: (868) 622-6628 / 0591
Email: delttopos@ec.europa.eu

Embassy of the French Republic
Tel: (868) 622-7447 / 2388 or
(868) 628-8633
Email: cad.port-d-espagne-
amba@diplomatie.gouv.fr

Embassy of the Federal Republic of Germany
Tel: (868) 628-1630 / 1632
Email: info@ports.diplo.de

High Commission for Great Britain and Northern Ireland
Tel: (868) 350-0444
Email: generalenquiries.ptofs@gov.tt

High Commission for the Republic of India
Tel: (868) 627- 7480 / 7481 / 4027
Email: hcipos@tstt.net.tt

High Commission for Jamaica
Tel: (868) 622-4995
Email: jhctnt@tstt.net.tt

Embassy of Japan
Tel: (868) 628-5991 / 5993
Email: embassyofjapan@tstt.net.tt

Embassy of the Kingdom of the Netherlands
Tel: (868) 625-1210 / 1722 / 2532
Email: por@minbuza.nl
Email: info@holland.tt

Embassy of the Kingdom of Spain
Tel: (868) 625-7930
Email: emb.trinidad@mae.es

Embassy of the United States of America
Tel: (868) 622-6371 / 6376
Web: trinidad.usembassy.gov

Embassy of the Republic of Venezuela
Tel: (868) 627-9821 / 9823-4
Email: embaveneztt@tstt.net.tt

OTHER CONTACTS

The Investor Sourcing & Facilitation Division
The Atrium, Don Miguel Road
Extension, El Socorro, Trinidad.
Tel: (868) 638-0038
Fax: (868) 675-9125
Web: www.investtnt.com
Web: www.investt.co.tt.
Email: info@investt.co.tt

Ministry of Tobago Development
Jerningham St, Scarborough
Tel: 639-2652

Ministry of Tourism
Levels 8 & 9 International
Waterfront Centre, #1
Wrightson Road, Port of
Spain, Trinidad.
Tel: (868) 625-0963, 623-9604
Fax: (868) 625-3894
Web: www.tourism.gov.tt

Ministry of Trade and Industry (Trinidad and Tobago)
Levels 11 to 17, Nicholas
Tower, 63-65 Independence
Square, Port of Spain, Trinidad.
Tel: (868) 623-2931-2934
Fax: (868) 627-8488 / 0002
Web: www.tradeind.gov.tt

Tourism Development Company (TDC) Ltd
Level 1, Maritime Centre, 29
10th Ave, Barataria, Trinidad.
Tel: (868) 725-7034
Fax: (868) 675-7338

Tobago News
Etech Mall, Sangsters Hill.
Tel: (868) 660-7107
Fax: (868) 639-5565
Email: ccngroupc@tstt.net.tt

ANR Robinson International Airport
Tel: (868) 639-0509

Cruise Ship Complex (Scarborough)
Tel: (868) 635-0934